A Journey in Eschatology

A Theological Novel

Richard P. Belcher

Cover Photography by Ravenel Scott

ISBN 1-883265-21-5

Richbarry Press

P.O. Box 302   **Columbia, SC 29202**
Phone: 803-750-0408
E-Mail: docbelcher@juno.com
Visit our web site at: www.richbarrypress.com

Printed in the Unites States of America

Contents

The Location in the Book
of the Various Eschatological Views
**(The page number of the beginning of the chapter
which contains the discussion is given.)**

Author's Preface

The study of eschatology (the doctrine of final things) may very well be the most difficult of the various areas of theological study! Yet, it seems, no other area has produced so many experts on the subject! Besides the numerous experts, there are other accompaniments to the study of eschatology, some which are positive and some which are negative.

The negatives would include <u>sensationalism</u> (the use of eschatology to create hair-raising, spine-tingling, extravagant, mind-blowing excitement); <u>exclusivism</u> (an elitist, restrictive barring from fellowship of other believers who might disagree with one in this area of theology); <u>apocalypticism</u> (a stressing of the prophetic books and passages and subjects of the Bible to the neglect of the other areas of theology); <u>a ministerial monism</u> (a preaching and teaching ministry that majors on eschatology supremely to the neglect of the other areas of theology); <u>a newsstand hermeneutics</u> (a study method that uses the recent events of the newspaper as an interpretive tool in understanding the prophetic portions of the Scriptures; <u>an ungodly hucksterism</u> (the use of the subject of eschatology to bring fame and some fortune to a writer); etc.

The positives would include the great <u>blessing</u> that comes from the study of the Word of God, whatever subject or portion of the word it might be, including prophecy, provided we study it with the proper attitude; the <u>challenge</u> of meditation on the providence of God in history, as He does control history past (some prophecies have already been fulfilled), and the <u>encouragement</u> of anticipating what He will bring to us and His creation in the future, as we consider those prophecies which are yet to be fulfilled; etc.

But does there not need to be some godly checks and balances to reign us in, in light of the many excesses in the study of eschatology, even those mentioned above? Should the church not be asking key questions, as she studies this doctrine today?

"What questions?" one might ask.

Is eschatology one of the major or minor doctrines of the Bible? If a minor doctrine (that is, one not essential for salvation), should we make it major in our emphasis, major as a test of fellowship, and major in our preaching and teaching ministry?

Is eschatology an easy subject, as some seem to imply, in that they are confident that they have everything figured out correctly already? Or is eschatology a very difficult subject? This is not to say that every difficult subject should be open to various interpretations, especially when the Scripture is clear and the doctrine is major. But if it is extremely difficult and not a major doctrine, should we not approach it with some divine wisdom and restraint as we move forward in our study and conclusions?

Is eschatology a subject, which we can understand by reading one book of the Bible, or one book by a prophetic writer, or is it a subject that requires a wide knowledge of the total revelation of God, both Old Testament and New Testament? Should a one book study of the subject give us authority to crown ourselves as eschatological know-it-alls and bash those who disagree with us as liberals, spiritual imbeciles, or worse?

Is the book of Revelation or Bible prophecy in its totality the place where a new believer should begin his or her study of the Bible, while neglecting the doctrine of God, Christ, the Holy Spirit, man, salvation, the Christian life, etc? Should the church today major on this area of theology, when members who have been professing believers for so many years, are so untaught in the above mentioned areas of theology?

The author has found that there are few theological subjects, which stir as much tension and animosity, when believers disagree with one another, than the subject of eschatology! Recognizing that, perhaps, places the writer in the place of being railed against as a heretic by some, or even accused by others of stirring division in the church. Actually, part of the purpose of this book is to relieve some of the tension and to unite rather than divide.

I would challenge all who read this work to seek to learn. I am fearful we often condemn the views of others in this area of eschatology without actually understanding their view point. I would encourage all, further, to practice a spiritual and intellectual honesty in seeking to be fair to other positions, and not erect strawmen, for the easier destruction of another's conviction.

Be assured that this is not a call for eschatological agnosticism, but a call for eschatological caution. That is, that we study eschatology with a painstaking carefulness, a cautious deliberateness, a meticulous attentiveness to details, along with a Christ-like humility towards others with whom we may not agree.

I do pray that the study of this book will lead us to that attitude and approach! Grace to us all as we study!

1

You Want Me to Write a Book?

If the reader will recall our previous journey (the search to understand something of the providence of God---though that subject certainly is incomprehensible), then it will be understood how worn and weary I was when facing the late summer of 1982. A full year had passed, and we had no hope of finding Dink's son, who had been kidnapped during the summer of 1981.

All leads had dried up, and, I must confess, I was not ready for another "journey" of any kind---not even one to go across the street or around the corner. But our sovereign and providential God, Who had guided us so clearly in our study of the book of Job, had other plans! And the journey in the study of eschatology (the study of future things), which I had been threatening to pursue, but had put off because I felt so unqualified to follow it, rose up to engulf me in a manner that I could not resist.

It all began when Mack Turnover got out of prison. Mack was the newsman who had been involved in the strawman episode in our *Journey in Inspiration*.[1] He had gone to prison for his illegal actions towards me, as he had sought to manufacture a more exciting story about the trouble over the doctrine of inerrancy on the campus of the seminary. But in the aftermath of it all, he was converted, and I had kept in touch, seeking to disciple him, even as he was serving his time. I hadn't seen or heard from him for a few months, but I did have word he was going to be released about this time. Little did I realize he would make a beeline for my door. And who should bring him to see me, but the Dink man!!

"Hey, Preacha!" he erupted, as I opened the door that early morning, hardly ready to see anyone.

"Look who I'se brought ta see ya!" he spoke again, rather proudly, as if he were the responsible party for disturbing me so early.

When I saw it was Mack, I greeted him warmly, and he returned the loving goodwill. Then after some reminiscing and some updating on his situation he broached the subject of his visit to me.

"Brother Ira, my father has become a Christian!" he spoke rejoicingly.

His father was a very wealthy man, who owned who-knows how many newspapers. He shared with us that his father had been saved through studying Bible prophecy! And now he was extremely interested in learning all he could on the subject.

I nodded with joy over this event, not even thinking it could have anything to do with me. Then Mack began to unfold slowly his plan for my part in a new journey for truth.

"Ira, my father is looking for someone to write a book on the subject of eschatology!" he finally blurted out. "Not a detailed work for scholars, but just a simple presentation for lay people!" he explained.

I nodded, not understanding yet that I was his target.

"He is so excited, and yet so confused, in light of the many views of the future according to the students of Bible prophecy, that he wants someone to detail all the views in an objective manner in a new book. He will finance this work from start to finish with a nice bonus thrown in to boot!"

And then it dawned on me.

"Are you asking ME to write this book?" I asked.

"Why not, Ira?" he replied pleadingly.

"Why not??" I snapped eager to argue with him. "I'll tell you why not! First, I am too busy. Second, I barely know what I believe about Bible prophecy. Third, I have never written a book. Fourth, I have no desire to write a book now. Fifth, I have different friends who hold to all these varying positions, and unless I defended their position, they might not be friends with me any more!"

I had added the last one, because though it may have sounded weak, there was some truth to it. Bible prophecy was a very controversial subject. Anyone who would write a book on his own view of eschatology would alienate in some manner many of those who held another position. I had seen it. I could remember men who had invited me to preach in their churches, and then when they found out I did not share their particular eschatological viewpoint to the nth degree, they canceled me.

But his offer was not just to write on my view, but to write on all views giving each one in an objective manner, not coming to any conclusion as to which one was the Biblical view. Didn't he realize that this would alienate everyone either because I had not taken any position, or on the other hand, because they thought I had misrepresented their position? I tried to explain all of this to him, but he would not take no for an answer.

Finally, I stated to him with firmness that I could not and I would not do it---period!!! But then he hit me with something that would make it almost impossible to say no!!

---

[1]See *A Journey in Inspiration* (Richbarry Press, 1998) by the same author.

Why Tear My Heart Open Anew?

As I had been talking, Mack reached into a satchel that he was carrying and pulled out a book---an old book! I had noticed it as I was laying down the law of my non-involvement in such a project, but thought nothing of it---until he handed it to me.

The book had a faded maroon cover with water spots in places. The title showed the book was definitely one on the subject of our discussion---*Dispensational Certainties---With Helpful Charts*. I thought, "So what!---an old book on Dispensationalism---big deal." Until I read the name of the author. It was Ira F. Pointer. You can imagine my shock, for I thought I was Ira F. Pointer. I had never known my parents for I had grown up in a children's home. I had never been adopted, and knew nothing of my real parents, not even their names. Any previous inquiries I had made for information had ended at a dead end. It seemed they had fallen off the face of the earth.

I must have looked at Mack inquisitively, because he began to offer me his deal.

'Brother Ira, if you will write this book on Bible Prophecy, my father will give his best investigative sources to seek to find out all they can about your parents. We will pursue their identity; are they still alive; what happened to them; why have you not been able to find them; and so on. I mean we will spare no time or expense to arrive at the truth so you can settle this matter once and for all.

I sat there stunned! I had given up all hope of ever finding any information about them, let alone to find them in person. I had given it over to the Lord and decided He did not want me to find them. I had dealt with all of those feelings some years ago when every search effort had failed. God had given me peace. Why should I allow these scars of childhood to be torn open once again? What good would it do if I found them? It seemed clear that they didn't want me then and probably didn't want me now, since they had covered their trail so completely when they had abandoned me. They had never sought to find me, so why should I seek to find them. How could such a search ever end in any joy?

My eyes began to water as the old feelings of loneliness and abandonment surged over me again. I recalled the nights in the children's home as I had cried myself to sleep because I did not have a father or mother like the other kids. I remembered feelings of jealousy in stores or other public places, when I saw children with their parents, and all I had were workers in the children's home, who were kind, but could never take the place of a mother. I recalled playing on local baseball teams as a young boy, and the wish which flooded my heart that I too could have a dad and mother who came to watch me play. I remembered in grade school that all the other kids had homes with a room of their own and all the latest toys and games. I had a room with several of us all together but few toys or games.

So why should I open all these sores once again? If this search was a success or a failure, it didn't seem like it could give me anything but more sorrow and feelings of rejection. So I replied rather sternly to Mack's offer.

"Mack, I do not fully understand your motive. I am a little disappointed that you would even spring this upon me! Surely, you must know what this puts me through. Is this just another calloused effort of a newsman to get something for himself (a book on eschatology) with no sensitivity to what he might do to others in the process (tear open my heart on matters God settled years ago)? Do you news people not have some sense of decency when it comes to disturbing other people's lives, just so you can get your way?"

He dropped his head in shame, so it seemed. My words were cutting him deeply, a clear evidence he was a believer. Then he apologized.

"I'm sorry, Pastor Ira! Please forgive me! I withdraw my father's offer. I will tell him we were very wrong even to approach you. I guess we news people do get carried away, and you have taught me a valuable lesson. I must be more sensitive to people and less bent on getting a story whatever the cost. In fact, I am reminded that this is what sent me to prison. Please forgive me."

I assured him of my forgiveness, and a few more words were spoken. Then he left, and the matter was settled. Or was it? I noticed that he had left the old faded book on the coffee table, and I found myself drawn to it. I picked it up and re-read the author's name---Ira F. Pointer.

What Is God's Will in This Matter?

As I reached over and picked up the old book once again, a sense of awe fell over me. Could these be the words which my father had penned decades ago! When he professed to be a Christian? When he was on fire for the Lord? When he was married to my mother? Before I was born? Or after I was born?

I opened the partly faded pages and found the title page to check the copyright date. It was dated 1951! My birth date was August 12, 1950, so if my father had written it, I was in the first year of my life when it was published. Could it be that he had written it during the days before I was born? I thrust the book away from me, placing it back on the table where Mack had left it. I cautioned myself that I could not let my feelings draw me into an emotional dead-end, which would yield no real spiritual fruit.

Then the phone rang once again. It was Dink.

"Hey, Preacha, can I say sumtin' and not hurt yer feelins?"

I couldn't imagine where he was heading.

"You'se was pretty tough on ol' Mack! Maybe da Lord wud want ta do a work in some body's life through dis search? Maybe save yer parents? Or who knows what? Remember what we'se been studien' on da sovereignty and providence of our great God?"

His words did cause me to remember my sovereign God! Perhaps this was from Him! Maybe He did want to teach me something through it! Maybe He wanted to bring one of His own unto Himself through this search? Maybe my mother and father were not Christians, and I could be the instrument of God to carry the gospel to them (though the book seemed to indicate that they were). But if they were, why would they abandon their son? Should I let my hurt and brittle feelings of the past, or a fear of the future keep me from doing the will of God, if this was a door of His opening? Could He not be my All and All and my victory over the results of someone's sin against me in the past, as well as my protector for the future?

After further discussions with Dink, I reached for the book again. I opened it and browsed through it quickly but with great interest. I noticed the language was impressive. And the charts were very well done. Could it be that the author of this book was still alive? Could it be that this man was my father? If so, where would he be now? Why did he cover his past? And how old would he be by now? My mind did some arithmetic. If he had been in his twenties or thirties when the book was written, then he would be in his sixties or so by now.

Other questions flooded my mind. Was he still in the ministry? Was he still married to my mother? If so, did they have other children? Why had he given me up? Was I sure I wanted to get into this search? And could I really write a book, especially in the middle of this parent search?

Then the phone disturbed my thoughts again. It was Mack.

"Pastor Ira, I want to apologize once again for my insensitivity!" he began.

I cut him off rather quickly.

"Mack, let me apologize also. I must now admit that probably I was a little oversensitive. I'm sure you can understand. And I think I have reconsidered your offer. I can't get any peace by refusing your request. Yes, I think the Lord would have me try to write the book---and I mean try. If the book is not acceptable to you, assure your father that he does not have to waste his money printing it. And if at any point in the process as I present chapters, tell him that he is free to notify me that I am not the man for the job, and we will end the writing effort as well as the search effort."

"Well, we're committed to you in the search for your parents whether the writing works out or not. We're not going to pull out on that pursuit. I already told my father that this had to be part of the bargain, and he agreed."

I gave a sigh of relief, because a burden had been lifted. Now, where would I begin in this project? They would do the parent-search, but I certainly had a difficult task.

Then Mack offered another bit of jarring information.

"Pastor Ira, I don't wish to hit you with another shock, and I wasn't going to tell you this just to get you to do the book. But since you have agreed to do so, I trust I can tell you that I think we are getting close to finding your mother! We think she's still alive and lives in Arkansas by herself. We are still looking for your father."

I couldn't help praising the Lord. Here I hadn't written a word, and the Lord, so it seemed, had allowed them to find my mother already. Perhaps that was a confirmation that I was doing His will.

Time would tell, for I reminded myself that it was neither success nor failure that could assure a man he was in the will of God.

Pre-mil, Post-mil, A-mil?

I went to bed that night pondering where I might begin in my pursuit of eschatology. As I couldn't sleep, even long after Terry, my wife, had drifted off, I rose to make some notes concerning a beginning. I wondered where to begin, and how basic to make the initial concepts of the book. I decided to begin at square one. I had been told not to write for scholars, but for lay people!

It was obvious to me that a key element in developing an eschatological view was the concept of a <u>millennium</u>. It was also true that the basic millennial concepts were known as:

> Pre-millennialism
> Post-millennialism
> A-millennialism

<u>First</u>, I would have to point out that the word *millennium* speaks *literally* of a period of one thousand years.

<u>Second</u>, I would show that interpreters do not always see the word as literal (a one thousand year period), but many see the term as representing *a symbolic era* (a long period of time).

<u>Third</u>, I would note that the above terms (Pre-mil, Post-mil, and A-mil for short) are used concerning the relationship of the Second Coming of Christ to one's concept of the millennium. I then set forth the following distinctions.

THE PREMILLENNIAL VIEW
OF THE SECOND COMING

The Pre-mil sees the one thousand-year period (millennium) as literal with Christ coming at the beginning of the millennium. He by His power brings in the millennium. I summarized and then drew a little chart as follows:

Christ will reign for a literal 1000 years
    in person on earth
Christ's Second Coming is at the
    beginning of the millennium
Thus He comes Pre to the millennium
    (before the millennium)
Thus the view is called the Pre-mil view
    Christ comes before the millennium

\/Christ comes at the BEGINNING of the millennium
\/
\/
<u>MILLENNIUM---1000 YEAR REIGN OF CHRIST</u>

Christ reigns on earth in complete control

THE POSTMILLENNIAL VIEW
OF THE SECOND COMING

The Post-mil view sees the one thousand-year period (millennium) as a period of time, but not a literal one thousand years. Christ will come at the end of the millennium. The power of God through the gospel brings in the millennium and Christ comes at the end of this period. I summarized and drew a chart as follows:

The power of God through the gospel
    brings in the millennium
        a long period of time on earth
        but not a literal 1000 years
Christ's Second Coming is at the
    end of the millennium
Thus He comes Post to the millennium
    (after the millennium)
Thus the view is called the Post-mil view
    Christ comes after the millennium

Christ comes at the END of the millennium V
                                                       V
                                                       V

<u>MILLENNIUM---A LONG PERIOD OF TIME</u>

The millennium is brought by God
through the power of the gospel

THE AMILLENNIAL VIEW
OF THE SECOND COMING OF CHRIST

The A-mil view says there is no literal millennium on earth (Christ will not reign literally or bodily on earth), but this period is a non-literal period extending from Christ's death to His Second Coming as He rules on His spiritual throne in heaven.   I summarized and drew a chart as follows:

The power of God at Christ's death
    brings His literal reign in heaven---
    thus this is not a literal 1000 years
    and this is not on earth but in heaven
Christ's Second Coming is at the end
    of the history of the present age
Thus there is no millennium on earth
    but a spiritual reign in heaven
Thus the view is called the A-mil view
    with "A" meaning no
    which means no earthly millennium

Christ reigns on a spiritual throne in heaven V
Christ comes at the end of this spiritual reignV
                                  V
<u>NO EARTHLY MILLENNIUM OF 1000 YEARS</u>

Christ's reign on His spiritual throne
    began at the cross
    and continues until He comes again

As I tried to doze off to sleep, after penning these thoughts and concepts (simple ones for so many, but I felt I had to begin there), I wondered what tomorrow might bring concerning the location of my mother? Many thoughts and questions danced through my mind.

How had they located her so quickly?

How would they approach her?
Had she changed her name also, like my father?
Would she have any desire to see me?
Would she know where my father was?

To be honest, I was somewhat frightened. I felt like I was about to board a rocket ship for the unknown. What else would they unearth in this quest to locate my birth parents? I even wondered if I had done the right thing in allowing this search to continue.

To divert my thoughts from these thoughts, I got up and made the following chart to summarize the three millennial views:

	Pre-Mil	**Post-Mil**	**A-Mil**
<u>Millennium</u> 1000 years	a literal 1000 year period	figurative-- not literal	figurative-- not literal
<u>Millennium</u> Where?	on earth	on earth	in heaven
<u>Millennium</u> Beginning?	at Second Coming	prior to Second Coming	at the cross of Christ
<u>Second Coming</u> Time of?	before millennium	after millennium	after Christ's heavenly reign
<u>What Follows</u> Second Coming?	the millennium	eternal state	eternal state

Pre-mil Dispensationalism?

The next morning, after breakfast with Ira, Jr. and Terry, I went to church needing to do so many things, but not certain I had the mind to do anything. As I was driving, it dawned on me for the first time I might be Ira, Jr. if my father were Ira, Sr.

Each time the phone rang that morning, I thought it might be Mack with some promised information. I had almost given up, when my secretary buzzed me and said, "Mack Turnover wants to speak to you." Gingerly I picked up the phone. Then came the words I had anticipated, but I was not sure I was ready to hear them.

"Pastor Ira, we think we have found your mother! Are you ready to fly to Arkansas?"

I stuttered and stammered trying to remember what I had planned that day. I'm sure I sounded like Porky Pig, and then I asked the simple question.

"How do I get there? Did you say fly? Mack, I can't afford to fly off to Arkansas on a hunch or hope!" I protested.

"Don't worry, preacher! Dink will fly with you, and we'll cover the bill. That's part of our agreement."

"Then you are pretty certain this is my mother? How do you know?" I asked before getting an answer to my first question.

"We're certain! No doubt about it!" he assured me.

"Have you talked to her?" I inquired further.

"No, we have only verified beyond any doubt that she is your mother. Approaching and talking to her is up to you," he informed me.

"So I fly out there with a hope that she will see me and talk to me?" I thought out loud? "What can you tell me about her?" I asked, hoping to be assured by some information, any information, that she might see me.

"She's in her sixties, and is a very wealthy lady!" he surprised me. "She owns a number of nursing homes!"

"Does she know I exist or that I am coming?" I blurted out almost in tears.

"No, we just found her. The rest is up to you!"

That afternoon Dink and I were on a plane out of Seminary City headed to Arkansas. We would land in Little Rock, and take a rented car an hour or so to the town where my supposed mother lived. As we flew I shared with Dink my previous study on Bible prophecy, and then added to that information as I spoke of the several kinds of pre-millennialism.

THE SEVERAL KINDS OF PRE-MILLENNIALISTS

I reminded Dink that the pre-mil view believed that Christ would come before the millennium and would set up then His one thousand year literal and bodily reign on this earth. I then reminded him (he may have known some of this previously) that not all pre-mils believed alike. They all believed the Second Coming of Christ would precede the millennium, but they didn't agree on other matters.

Actually, there were three kinds of pre-mils we would discuss: the dispensational pre-millennialists, the historic pre-millennialists and the covenantal pre-millennialists.

The Dispensational Pre-Millennialists

This group of pre-mils believed that God had two peoples with two plans for these two groups of people. The two peoples were Israel and the Church. Israel was the Old Testament people of God, and the Church was the New Testament people of God.

God's plan for Israel, the Old Testament people, was an earthly kingdom, and when Christ came He offered such a kingdom to them. If the Jews of Christ's day had received Him as their Messiah and King, he would have set up His earthly kingdom immediately. But they did not receive Him. They rejected Him and crucified him. Thus God rejected them for a period of time, which period is known as the times of the Gentiles. During that time God put His plan for Israel in cold-storage and began the work of His Church---the calling out of a group of Gentiles.

In the passing of time the Gentile nations would reject Christ fully also, as the Church would become apostate in the latter days of its history. Only a remnant would remain faithful to Christ in those final days of human history. This faithful group of mostly Gentile believers on earth at the end of history would be raptured (caught up from the earth) at the beginning of what is known as the tribulation period, a time span of seven years. God would then turn once again to the Jews, and a great multitude of them will be saved during this seven year period.

This tribulation period will be not only a time of the conversion of the Jews, but also the hour that Christ judges the Christ-rejecting Gentiles, as the saved Gentiles (the Church) will be in heaven with Christ at this time. The Antichrist will be unleashed upon the earth. He will take three and a half years to gain power, and then the last three and a half years, he will be in full control on earth until Christ comes to defeat him and set up His literal kingdom.

Thus dispensationalists see such an antithetical distinction between Israel and the Church, that they cannot be on earth at the same time. They believe that the rapture of believers will take place at the beginning of the tribulation period. Their conviction is known as the pre-tribulational rapture view, or for short, the pre-trib rapture.

I sought to draw another chart to illustrate this idea:

```
          Rapture of
          the Church-------------Second
              V                  Coming
              V        7 yrs     V
              Λ                  V
              Λ                  V  1000 year reign
              Λ                  V  of Christ
CHURCH AGE    |    TRIBULATION   V  MILLENNIUM
```

1. The Jews reject Christ prior to the church age.
2. God turns to the Gentiles to call out the Church.
3. God's plan for the Jews is put in cold storage.
4. God raptures out His church at the beginning of the tribulation period---pre-trib rapture.
5. God works once again with the Jews, saving a multitude of people from their race.
6. The Antichrist is turned lose on the earth for the tribulation period of 7 years.
7 The tribulation period is described in the greater part of the book of Revelation.

Then before I knew it, we were landing in Little Rock!!

Is Your First Name, Ira?

We picked up our rental car after deplaning, and headed for our destination outside of the city. Dink was driving, and I must admit, I was not much of a conversationalist. We came into the small town about an hour later, and had no trouble finding the nursing home, and it was clear that Mack's people were thorough in giving directions and all other matters. We had been told to go to this home and ask for Miss Thelma Fife.

Her last name was Fife? I hadn't noticed that previously. This seemed to give further evidence that she might be my mother, for my middle name was Fife, and it was a common practice in some places to use a maiden name in the naming of a child. I got out of the car and made my way to what appeared to be a front door of this rather sprawling nursing home. The butterflies were flying more like bumble bees in my stomach, and I even felt a little nauseous. I took a deep breath, and stepped inside to face a receptionist.

"I-I-I wonder if I could see Miss Thelma Fife?" I asked as politely as I had ever couched a question.

"Can I tell her who's calling?" she asked as my tongue seemed to stick as if glued tightly to the roof of my mouth.

"Uh," I stuttered, searching for words. I don't know why I hadn't thought of this moment. Surely she would not see just any one who walked in.

And then I had the answer to her question.

"Tell her that I was in town, and that I think we might be related, and I just wanted to see if that was so!"

I had told her the truth, and at the same time had not divulged the delicate nature of my visit. The receptionist asked me to sit down for a moment, and promised that Miss Fife would see me shortly. I was glad it was a small town. Relatives meant something here in these areas. Walk into a large city office, and you might get the cold shoulder for any request except one relating to business.

And then the hour arrived! The receptionist said I could go through a door at the end of the hall, and she would see me. I have never had such a long walk in all my life, but it wasn't long enough. What would I say? How could I handle this matter in a proper manner. What if she was not my mother?

I opened the door, and she rose from her desk, which was located in a very impressive office. She smiled at me, and I felt somewhat relieved, but then I knew I had to speak. She was a very beautiful lady, in about her mid-sixties, dressed not like a small town girl, but with some elegance. She spoke with precision and clarity.

"The receptionist said you thought you might be related to me!" she began with a smile.

"Yes, I think I might be. In fact, I really hope I might be." I spoke with all seriousness, and she seemed to catch the tone of my voice.

"Are you related to the Fifes or to the Scrantons?" she asked again.

Then I saw my chance to lead her into this matter without offense, and so I proceeded.

"I think I am related to the Fifes and the Pointers!" I said slowly and carefully. Evidently the Fifes and the Scrantons were her mother and father's families. The

Pointers were my father's family, and I knew that if she was my mother, she had to understand something unique was taking place.

The smile on her face vanished too as she queried, "The Pointers? What makes you think I know any Pointers?"

"My last name is Pointer!" I replied. "And my middle name is Fife! Does that mean anything to you?"

Then it was her turn. "And your first name is Ira?" she asked. I noticed some tears beginning to flow.

"Can you prove that?" she queried kindly.

I showed her my driver's license, and when she saw my birthday date on it, that settled it. She turned her back to me, and took a few moments to gather herself, not knowing exactly what to do next. Turning to face me, she made a request through her tears.

"You are my son! Would it be proper for a mother to hug her boy, whom she hasn't seen for thirty years?"

No answer was ever given! We simply embraced with both of us crying as if we would never stop.

As we hugged she said, "I have dreamed of this day, but I never thought it would come. I had given up hope of ever seeing you again!"

I acknowledged that those were my same feelings---that I had wept many evenings longing to have a mother, not knowing who she was or where she was, or if I would ever meet her.

"I can see we have so much to discuss. I hope you have come to stay several days? You can stay with me. I have plenty of room."

And then the questions began to fly from both sides. Yes, there was so much to catch up on. I was certainly interested to learn where she had been all these years. And what about my father? Did she know where he was?

Who Can Understand God's Ways?

With this news she immediately called her secretary and instructed her to close down her office for the day. I introduced her to Dink, who had been waiting in the reception area, and we went to a restaurant for supper. We talked about her life first, and these are the facts she shared with me.

This small community in Arkansas was her hometown. When she was very young she had met a preacher named Ira Franklin Pointer, my father. It was clear now, that though we had the same middle initials, I was not a junior. The original Ira Pointer was on fire for the Lord, even at this youthful age. She had been saved when she was in her early teens, and this young man of God swept her off her feet romantically and spiritually. They were married, and then set off for seminary in Texas. Then they learned she was pregnant, and the home was doubly happy in expectation of my birth. I was born on August 12, 1950, and the couple rejoiced greatly over their new son. My father's potential was recognized by all, as he even published a book at that young age. Yes it was the book that Mack had given to me.

Then in the next two years something very sad happened. My father began to lose his faith. It is not that he turned his back on Christianity immediately and completely, but that he began to embrace a more liberal view of the Bible. He doubted the verbal inspiration of the Scriptures, the miracles in the Bible, the virgin birth of

Christ, the need of personal salvation, the sinfulness of man, etc. With that evolution in his doctrinal thinking, he also became very difficult to live with as he adopted a much more liberal lifestyle.

Understandably they began to have tension in the home, as he came and went as he pleased, and she never knew where or with whom he had been. Finally, he dropped out of school, and became something of a reprobate in mind, attitude and action. Eventually, she couldn't take it any longer, so she left him and came back to her home, bringing me with her. But her home situation with her parents wasn't good either.

Her parents were old and very poor, and she had to live with them. They were not able to take care of me, so she could get a job, thus her life was to care for them and me as best she could. She took in some other elderly people so she could support us, and thus also began the nursing home business. It was a very difficult life, under these circumstances, but she was making it, and she was also able to provide for her young son.

Then a few months later, my father came to the house in a rage and took me away. He had no legal authority to do so, but that did not matter to him. He was so bitter and godless at this point, that his main concern was to hurt her. I was not the issue. It was all to vent his anger towards her for leaving him. And though she searched and searched through the years, she never saw him or heard of me or my whereabouts again---until today. Thus, she assured me that it was not her choice to give me up or to lose me for all those years, but the choice of my father.

When I asked what had happened to him, she answered she did not know. He changed his identity, and it was like Ira Pointer had never existed. To her knowledge he had never contacted even a single family member. They had been just as puzzled through the years as she was as to his existence and place of dwelling. And she had no idea where I was through those years.

Then I filled her in on my life. I told her of growing up in a children's home, which brought her more tears of sorrow for me. I told her of coming to know Christ, and then of His call to me to preach, and that I was now pastoring in the southeast. I told her of Terry, and of Ira, Jr. Again, she wept profusely as we spoke.

When she asked how I had found her, I told her of Mack Turnover and his conversion and offer to me to write a book for his father. She smiled as I shared that part of the offer was to find her and my father, if I would do it.

Then I asked her about her spiritual life since the sad events of her younger days. She stiffened and hardened and replied, as she looked at the floor.

"Son, I have given my life to these nursing homes. I have become a very respected and wealthy business woman, not only in this town, but statewide. I must confess that those early events have hardened me against church and Christianity. After a few months of praying and seeking the Lord, asking him to bring you back, I gave up. I have not lived immorally, but have poured me life into these homes to keep my sanity. Maybe I was wrong, but that was the only thing that brought me any comfort---to serve others. Yes, I turned inward, and had no desire to be with the hypocrites at church. I felt I could never trust another Christian. Maybe I was wrong, but that's the way it was." She spoke boldly and with a hardened attitude.

Then Dink spoke up.

"Mam, you may not know it, but ya got da finest son any lady could ever have or hope for! You'se can trust him!!! He's da one dat led me to Jesus. He's da one who's keepin' me an' my wife goin right now---dat is, as He keeps pointin' us ta Jesus and da providence of God. Jus' about a year ago, my little two year old son was kidnapped, and as far as we know, he's dead. But your son has kept us goin' on fer Jesus. All dose other folks out der may have failed ya, but Jesus won't! And now ya got yer son back. Don't ya tink its time ta thank Jesus fer dat, and come back ta him. Was ya saved to begin with dose years ago?"

She looked at me through tears, and then said with a smile, "You've got quite a convert and sidekick there!! I can tell, he's real!! Son, I guess I needed someone like you or Dink in my life those years ago to encourage me, like you have encouraged Dink. No one gave me any encouragement. I know its no excuse, but I was on my own with parents to care for, and I had no desire to be with people, who instead of showing love for me, condemned me for being divorced, as if it was my fault. Do you think God can forgive me for those years when I built a shell around myself, isolating myself from people, for fear of being hurt further from their pettiness and lack of concern for one who was really hurting? And, yes, in my heart I longed to find you, but, again, I didn't want to find you lest the scars of the past would be torn open and my fortress of indifference and self-centered comfort be destroyed as well. Does that make any sense, not that I am excusing myself?"

Then we all prayed and cried again. I didn't think Dink would ever stop praying or bawling. Then my mother prayed. It was a prayer of repentance and thanksgiving, asking Christ to forgive her. It was amazing how the grace of Christ could wipe away the hardened layers of years of bitter sorrow!

8

The Historic and Covenantal Pre-mil?

Dink and I stayed two nights with my mother, and it was as if we had never been apart. When she took us to the airport, she promised with eagerness that she would visit me, as she was so anxious to meet Terry and young Ira.

Before leaving her, I asked if there was any suggestion she could give us in seeking to find my father. She admitted that she had no reason to find him or see him again, but she understood my desire. Yet at the same time, I think she was honest, when she said she had no idea how to reach him. For thirty years it had been as if he was dead!

I asked about relatives who might help, and she guaranteed that none of them knew anything either. I asked about unique hobbies, and she said it depended upon which way he had gone. If he had come back to the Lord, he would be a lover of the Word of God and the ministry of it to hungry souls. But if that had been the case, he surely would have emerged from his hiding, seeking to make things right with those he had wronged. On the other hand, if he was still in sin, only God knew where to find him. He might even be dead! She spoke those words with some conviction, indicating perhaps that if he were dead, she would be neither surprised nor disappointed. Perhaps that would bring some closure to her situation.

"Don't you know, Ira, that I live with the thought that someday he may emerge, wanting to make things right. What would I do then? I still love the man I married. That man was so godly and loving and kind. I do not love the man he became. But I am not sure I could even enter a relationship with the man I married after all these years, if it was even possible that he could return to that. He still wouldn't be the man I married. The broken dreams we held together are gone. The hope for any future is shattered. A life of love and commitment has been devastated by his actions. How do you erase thirty years of betrayal and deception? I would rather live alone than try to re-establish a dead relationship on the basis of an uncertain hope!"

She was emphatic and strong at this point, and I could understand why. Perhaps that attitude was what had allowed her to endure, or perhaps that is the attitude that developed through her endurance over the years.

As the plane lifted off the runway, I wondered what would be our next move. Perhaps Mack and his men were already in pursuit. The world was such a big place, but surely a man cannot hide forever!

I turned and asked Dink if he wanted to do some study in Bible prophecy, and he agreed. So I suggested that we look at the historic pre-mil view.

The Historic Pre-millennial View

I reminded us that the dispensational pre-mil view was very strong in believing in two people (Israel and the church) and two plans for these people. But I informed us both that this was not the case with the historic pre-mil conviction.

That position would see that God has one people and one plan for His people. God has always from the time of the fall of Adam been saving a people, and they all are part of the one body of Christ. There is a distinction between Israel and the Church, but not the antithetical distinction as seen by the dispensationalists. In fact, the historic view would see two Israels---the national Israel and the spiritual Israel. Even in the Old Testament, there was an Israel within an Israel. The multitudes of Jews made up national Israel, while the saved Jews made up the spiritual Israel.

Then when one comes into the New Testament, the Gentiles who become Christians become part of the spiritual Israel, which is that one body of believers of all ages that God is saving by His grace. At the same time during this New Testament period, the unbelieving Jews are part of ethnic Israel because they are descendants of Abraham, but they are not spiritual Israel because of their unbelief in the Messiah. We could chart it like this:

Israel # One	Israel # Two
All those who are the physical descendants of Abraham, that is, ethnic Jews, who have no part of the body of Christ on this basis alone.	All who are the spiritual descendants of Abraham, both Jews and Gentiles, who make up the one people of God, the one body of Christ.

Thus in a sense the historic pre-mil believes in two peoples, but in only one spiritual people, the Church, while the dispensationalist believes in two spiritual peoples, Israel and the Church.

This is part of the reason the dispensationalist believes in a pre-trib rapture. God has two different plans for these two peoples, and only one of God's plans is in effect on the earth at a time. I charted that as follows:

The Dispensational Pre-Mil View of the Rapture

Plan # One	Plan # Two
This plan of God is in effect for the Jews during the OT period and during the tribulation..	This plan of God for the Church is in effect in the New Testament period.

Thus since God moves back to Plan Number One in the tribulation period, the Jews must be the focus. Therefore the church is taken out at the beginning of the tribulation period as God moves back to Plan Number One.

The Historic Pre-mil View of the Rapture

One Plan of God for All of History
Whether it be in the OT period or the NT period or the tribulation period, God has only one plan---to save one people from Jews and Gentiles and all races. Thus the church is not raptured at the beginning of the tribulation period, for God will continue to do in the tribulation period what he was doing in the OT and the NT period---saving a people. The historic pre-mil would allow that the end of the age may result in the salvation of a great number of Jews, but they will be part of the one body of Christ, as was and is the saved of all ages. Thus the tribulation period will be a continuation of what God has been doing since the fall of Adam, and the people of God will go through the tribulation, just as many of the people of God have faced tribulation throughout all their history in both the Old Testament and New Testament periods.

Dink was getting tired by now, but I wanted to cover one more area---the Covenantal Pre-mil view.

The Covenantal Pre-mil View

This conviction is really a further development of the historic pre-mil position, in that it is a Calvinistic presentation. I charted it as follows:

God's Everlasting Covenant of Grace
Is the umbrella which is over all of history
Whereby God governs His world and works out His plan
according to the Covenant of Grace
whereby God the Father has chosen a people to be His own
by His sovereign grace from eternity past
whereby God the Son has been given this people
to be their Redeemer and Lord
to die for them in particular manner
whereby God the Holy Spirit has agreed to apply the work
of the Son to this chosen people
regenerating them and giving them repentance and faith
and working in them the full work of salvation
thus keeping them through life and into eternity

/   OR ONE MIGHT PUT IT LIKE THIS   \
/   The Everlasting Covenant of Grace   \
/   as the umbrella of God over history   \
| as He saves this people by His sovereign grace |

|

HISTORY
FROM CREATION TO THE NEW EARTH
FROM GENESIS TO REVELATION

Again, I emphasized that this view, the Covenantal Pre-millennial view, was the Calvinistic presentation of the historic pre-mil position, but by now I had lost Dink. He was against the window snoring lightly. I did in my own mind make some notations.

1. As important as Bible prophecy might be, it is not an essential and major doctrine of the church.

2. Believers must learn that there will be differences among Christians in their eschatological views

3. Believers must learn to distinguish between the major and the minor doctrines of the church.

4. Believers must also learn to major on the major doctrines and minor on the minor doctrines, and never major on the minors nor minor on the majors.

5. Believers must never make a particular view of eschatology a test of fellowship.

As my eyes fell shut, I concluded that maybe God had given me, during these few days, a lesson concerning the place of eschatology in the Christian life. Not wanting to deny its place as part of the revelation of God to us in His Word, and not wanting to deny its great blessing to the believer, I still had to conclude that it was not as important as some men had made it.

I remembered that as I had spoken with my mother those few hours, eschatology was not the main focus of our hearts. The main focus was the grace of God to sinners, and the work of Christ in redemption for us.

Again I sought to chart these two positions:

	Dispensational Pre-mil	**Historic Pre-mil**	**Covenantal Pre-mil**
Time of Rapture	Pre-trib	Post trib	Post trib
Number of People	Two---Israel and the Church	One--- Church	One--- Church
Number of Plans	Two---Israel and the Church	One--- Church	One--- Church
Calvinist or Arminian	Variety--- could be either	Variety--- could be either	Calvinist

9

Are All Post-mils Liberal?

I arrived home that Saturday evening just in time to go to bed, and rise the next morning to preach. I was glad that I usually made a practice of being ahead in my sermon preparation. But the real excitement was not my message that day, but the rejoicing of God's people as I shared with them the past few days. And I must confess, Dink got in his licks too, in fueling the atmosphere of joy and victory.

That afternoon, Mack called, and there was more praise to God as I shared the victory with him. Then I asked him a question, and he had one for me in return.

"Well, have we got any leads on my father?" I asked with greater confidence now.

"We had a man in California that we thought might be him, but it turned out to be a false alarm. There's another man who has stepped forward claiming to be your father, but I don't hold much hope in him. Your father, after hiding all these years, would not be as eager, its seems to me, to come forward now. Now my question for you! How are you coming on the book?"

I informed him that I had worked through the material for several chapters, and would continue to do so. He assured me that he was not pushing me, nor was his father, but they were just eager to see the subject covered.

And so was I! In fact, I was so eager, that I spent Monday afternoon working on the next step of my study--- the various post-mil views of eschatology.

The Liberal Post-mil View

This view was strong at the beginning of the twentieth century as it rested on the basis of the rationalism of the nineteenth century. That period had concluded that they could not believe anything that could not be confirmed by man's reason.

Thus, there came into the church the search for the historical Jesus. The liberal scholars had concluded that the miracles of the Bible could not be true, nor could the supernatural in the Bible be believed, so they tried to find Jesus in the purely natural rather than the supernatural realm. Understandably they came up with a natural Jesus who was devoid of His deity, His divine purpose, and His power to save sinners. The best He could be was some kind of a human example to men.

Thus there came also the belief that man was moving up the evolutionary ladder, getting better by the century. In fact, this group of liberal thinkers no longer believed in the uniqueness of man by creation, nor in the ruination of man by sin, nor in the salvation of man by the blood of a divine Christ, nor in the power of God to intervene in history. They were convinced that man was caught in the upward and unfolding power of evolution, which would pull him to the top of an existence which would bring an unparalleled golden age of never-ending peace, prosperity with all of it coming not from God, but from man's wisdom and power.

But this view took a beating in World War I when it was evident again that a creature like man, who could be guilty of such inhumanities to his fellow man, was not soon approaching the golden age. But liberal thinkers rallied once again, and World War I was coined as the war that would end all wars---that is, until World War II came. And then the Korean conflict. And then the Vietnam saga. Thus the liberal view of an emerging superman in a super era was all but dead, and the younger generation began to question all the thoughts, and ideas and motivations of the older generation.

I noted that many believers in the first part of the century tended to put all post-mils in the same boat, concluding that they all must be liberals. But that was a wrong conclusion then, and it is a wrong conclusion now. There was prior to this century, and there has emerged during this century, several strands of the post-mil position in the camp of those committed to the full authority of the Bible.

The Biblically-based Post-Mil Views

By Biblically based I was seeking to recognize those systems of eschatology which sought to set forth a view from the exegesis and exposition of the Bible, not from the basis of a lost unbelieving mind. These men held to all of the evangelical doctrines of the faith.

The Historic Post-mil View

Even back in the previous centuries, there were sincere, godly, Bible believing scholars and Bible teachers who held to the Post-mil position. In its simplicity (we will go deeper into this view later---we are just seeking to get a general introduction here) this conviction stated the following:

1. God will bring in the fullness of the millennium or kingdom by the preaching of the gospel in this present age.

2. The gospel that will produce the final age is the one-and-only gospel based on the divine person and work of Jesus Christ as the redeemer for sinners.

3. The gospel will not bring the conversion of all men, but will produce a gradual growth, bringing in time salvation to a great multitude of the population of the earth, so that the world will be under the sway of the power of Jesus Christ and His kingdom, even though He will not be present during this final kingdom age.

4. The final form of the kingdom will be a period of great spiritual and economic prosperity as the result of the power and expanding influence of the truth of God.

5. The time of the kingdom or millennium will not necessarily be a literal one thousand years, but a lengthy period of time. There is a sense in which the kingdom is present now, possessing a nature and power of growth.

6. Christ will return to this earth at the end of the final age of the millennium, thus this position is called the Post-mil (after the millennium) view of the return of Christ.

7. At the end of this period, which is known as the millennium, Christ will return visibly to the earth, the dead both saved and unsaved will be resurrected to stand before the final judgment seat of God, which will be followed by the new heavens and the new earth.

8. There are people from varying theological backgrounds who hold to this position, but it has been in the past and continues to be today a position held by many Calvinists, who would argue that it is a position which recognizes the great power of the gospel, and the clear purpose of God for this earth---that all knees must bow before the Lord Jesus Christ.

9. The reader should also note that there is a world of difference between this view and the liberal post-mil view, a difference as great as between day and night. It is a certain shame, regardless of one's millennial position, that some in church history and even today have not recognized this.

Then as I was noting that there was one more post-mil view that I needed to mention, a position known as theonomy, I was interrupted by a visitor who was totally unexpected, and maybe not fully welcome!

10

Are You Going to Tell Me or Not?

I was not eager to see a visitor at this moment, for I still had an area of the post-mil view to consider. But when my secretary informed me there was a man to see me, who was named Samuel Seavers, I was even less eager to see him. He was the twin brother of James Seavers, alias Durwood Girvin, and they both had been very troublesome to me in days past.[1]   He too had gone to jail, along with Mack Turnover, for their illegal deeds in the inerrancy battle.

Reluctantly I told her to show him in, and I had every expectation to dismiss him as quickly as possible, so I could get back to my eschatological pursuit.

"My dear beloved studious gracious brother in Christ," he proclaimed with a giant smile on his face, and the best voice of friendliness he could muster.

I said hello, shook his hand, and asked him how I could help him.

"Oh, my dear boy, 'tis not you who can help me, but 'tis I who can help you, unless you continue to show that deep and brooding resentment towards one who comes to bring you deep and tantalizing sensations of joy!"

I wasn't aware that I was that unfriendly, nor was I aware of any way possible he could bring me any joy. I had seen his and his brother's hypocrisy before, and was not in any mood to play games with him.

"Oh, how can you help me?" I asked pointedly.

"I understand that you are looking for your father? Is that correct?" he asked.

"Yes, that is correct!" I stated. "How do you know, and what do you know that pertains to this subject?" I spoke bluntly with some clear displeasure in my voice.

"Tut, tut, my boy! Be patient, and I will with my nimble wit and matchless vocabulary unfold before you a golden summer of marvelous fertility concerning your father, and what I can do to release from your soul this burden of barren regrets which now plague you."

I wanted to order him out of my office for his arrogant attitude, especially in light of his previous dishonesty, but I wondered if maybe he might have something. I couldn't gamble on dismissing a possible lead, although I couldn't even begin to imagine how he could help me.

"Okay, get on with it!" I ordered him gently.

"Now that is so much better, and I trust that before I am finished that your first faint trace of irritation toward me will become a fever of enthusiasm!"

I rolled my eyes, and shook my head, and I guess he saw I was not developing "a fever of enthusiasm."

"Seriously, my dear brother, I met your father years ago, and I may have even met you!" he said in simple words.

"You what?" I shot back with unbelief!

"Yes, when I was a lad, about thirty years ago, your father preached a revival meeting for our church under the name of Ira F. Pointer. He had with him a small child about two years of age, and my guess is that the child was you!"

"Can you prove that?" I asked, knowing he was telling a good story, but I was not certain of his credibility.

"Will this prove it to you?" he challenged, as he stuck a picture in front of my face.

Sure enough, there was a man and a little boy! The picture was somewhat faded with age, so I studied it carefully. I had not seen any pictures of my childhood at that age, so I squinted, thinking maybe I could scrutinize each person's characteristics in a better manner.

It appeared that my father was an average sized individual, as far as height, but in weight he was rather thin---about 150 pounds. He had a face with more of a rectangular shape, sharp facial features, with penetrating eyes. He had a full head of dark black hair. The little boy certainly had my characteristics, and I had a tendency to believe the picture was real!

"Where was this revival?" I now demanded with a building "fever of enthusiasm."

"Ah, so you are now friendly and interested in Samuel Seavers' help. But now see upon my face the faint tremor of light-hearted amusement. Why should I be moved with compunction to continue for you my entrancing melody of helpful thoughts, when you possessed such a haunting and horrible sense of insecurity towards me at first as I came only to help you?"

I didn't want to be unchristian about the matter, but I knew of no other way to deal with such a flake. So I was about to get to the point and show him my fist, though he probably had calculated I would not, when Dink walked in. There was no one Seavers feared as much as he did Dink.

"Has ya got some trouble here, Preacha?" he asked as he looked Seavers over with his most intimidating stare.

"Well, that is up to Mr. Seavers!" I replied.

"So whadayasay, Mr. Seavers? Has we got trouble here?"

Immediately Seavers gave me the answer I wanted.

"This picture was taken in Joplin, Missouri in the summer of 1952. And that is all I know about the matter!"

he stated quickly and eagerly. Then he was gone, and I was glad!

I wondered to myself, why did he have to be such a jerk? Why couldn't he have come with kindness and in sincerity to help me with the information I would have so warmly welcomed. Why did he have to make an arrogant production out of it all? Why did he have to play games with no sensitivity of what I was experiencing? Where was an apology or spirit of repentance for what he had done to me previously?

But he had left the picture! So Dink and I studied it over and over, passing it back and forth between us, and then looking at it together.

Dink kept saying, "Ya knows, Preacha, it looks like somebody I knows!"

But when I asked him who, he had no answer. I reminded him that the picture was taken a long time ago, and the man, if alive today, could look entirely different, especially if he sought to change his identity, as it seems he obviously did.

"Yeah, but I still tink I met him somewheres at sometime!"

But then again, he couldn't identify him. I concluded he probably hadn't, and if he had, it wasn't when I was around, because the man looked totally unfamiliar to me.

"What next?" Dink asked.

"Somebody needs to go to Joplin!" I concluded.

---

[1]See some of the previous "Journey" books by the same author and publisher. For James Seavers, alias Durwood Girvin, see *A Journey in the Spirit* (1997), and for Samuel Seavers see *A Journey in Inspiration* (1998).

11

Theonomic Post-millennialism?

After talking with Mack, Dink and I were off to Joplin, Missouri. I had also spoken with my mother, and she informed us that my father's closest friend in seminary was a man from the same city. His name was Andrew Townsend, and he was pastoring in Joplin about the time my father left her. She had called him when my father left with me, but Rev. Townsend claimed he had not seen or heard from him. Mack then checked and found out that he was still living, though retired from the ministry. He insisted that I go, because if he knew anything he might talk to me, rather than some reporter or detective.

While we waited in the airport and then as we flew, we sought to finish the area of our study in theonomic post-millennialism. I made the following notes:

1. Obviously the theonomic post-mils had much in common with the historic post-mils, as follows:

    a. *God will bring the fullness of the kingdom by the preaching of the gospel in this age.*

    b. *The power of the preaching of the Word of God will produce the fullness of the kingdom.*

    c. *Not all men will be converted, but there will be a gradual growth of the kingdom by the conversion of a great multitude of the population.*

d. *Thus, the world will be under the sway of the power of Jesus Christ and His kingdom, even though He will not be present during the millennium itself.*

e. *The time of the kingdom or millennium will not be a literal one thousand years, but a lengthy period of time.*

f. *Christ will return to this earth at the end of the millennium, thus, this position is called the post-mil view of the return of Christ (after the millennium).*

But I noted for Dink that the post-mil theonomist would go further than this. The word "theonomy" comes from two Greek words, *theos* and *nomos*, the words for God and law. But more must be emphasized in this view than just these two words.

The emphasis of theonomy begins with God and His covenantal relationship with His people (thus theonomy is one form of covenant theology, though not all covenant people are theonomists). Part of that relationship understands that when His people are faithful in obedience to His requirements found in His law and/or His Word, He will bless them. If they are not faithful, He will not bless them. Though the word "blessing" refers to many areas, one of the primary areas is the certain success of God's program to bless the nations of the earth through His covenant people, as and only as they are faithful to Him.

The emphasis of theonomy, as indicated even in the above paragraph and in the word nomos, also places a strong emphasis on the law of God. It is the standard of obedience for God's people, as it is the reflection and mirror of His nature. It is not some arbitrary set of rules and laws, but a true reflection of His nature. Theonomists reject any idea that might suggest that the law of God ceased to be the standard of God's people as God's plan moved into the New Testament era. His law is eternal because it reflects His eternal nature. Thus God's people of all ages are responsible to obey it, not for salvation, but as the covenant people of God. Only then will they know the blessings of God upon them, and the advancement of His kingdom.

The emphasis of theonomy also included the concept that God's ethical standards in His Old Testament law are binding as a model for every nation of the world. God's law is the only divinely given law, and it is binding upon every man and nation of the earth in every era and period of history. God's law, therefore, is also the divine standard for every judicial system and law court of every land for penal sanctions and decisions.

At this point Dink popped up with a proper comment.

"Wow, Preacha, dat principle is gonna need some explanation!!!"

I agreed that it did, and we would come to that explanation later. But for now we were trying to get a general understanding of each view in its raw simplicity, so that when we came to fuller discussions, we would not be scratching our heads and asking, "What is a post-mill?" etc. So I urged him for now to seek to understand and memorize the basic principles of each group.

I reminded him that thus far we had dealt with the various kinds of Pre-mils (dispensational pre-mils, historic pre-mils, and covenantal pre-mils) and also the Post-mils (the liberal post-mils, the historic post-mils and the theonomic post-mils). I warned him to expect me to ask him to define any of these views at any time I might ask him.

As Dink rested, I constructed a chart to set forth the various post-mil views:

	Liberal Post-mil	Historic Post-mil	Theonomic Post-mil
Inspiration of the Bible	No	Yes	Yes
Gospel will Change the World	No	Yes	Yes
Christ comes at the end of Millennium	In Spirit	In body	In body
Calvinistic view	No	Usually	Yes
All will be converted	No	No	No
A literal 1000 yrs	No	No	No
Strong emphasis on OT Law in millennium	No	No	Yes

When I finished this chart, I too rested for the remainder of the trip, which included a stop in a connecting city. My heart pounded as we left the airport in Joplin. I tried to be a realist about finding my father as easily as I had found my mother. She had not sought to cut herself off from society. Nonetheless, there was some excitement that we might learn something which we did not know before.

We took a cab to Andrew Townsend's home, asked him to wait for us, and then walked up the long sidewalk to a well-kept two storied house in the older part of the city. Dink knocked on the door while my heart felt like it was knocking like a car on low-octane gasoline. An elderly lady answered the door, and the look on her face was shock and bewilderment as I spoke.

"Good afternoon, Mam! I wonder if we could see Rev. Townsend. I'm Rev. Ira Fife Pointer!"

Her mouth dropped open about a mile! She stood frozen for a few seconds staring at me as if she had seen a ghost.

"I'm sorry, Mam, I didn't mean to startle or frighten you. I'm Ira F. Pointer, and I am trying to locate my father, Ira Franklin Pointer, and I've been told Rev. Townsend knew my father. Could I speak with him a few minutes?"

Then all she would say, over and over, as she looked at me, was "I can't believe it!!! I just cannot believe it.!!!"

It was obvious that we had stumbled onto something!

Is This Another Dead End?

I felt badly as we stood before this lady, probably Mrs. Townsend, as she seemed spooked because of my presence. I sought to apologize, but nothing seemed to help her. Finally, a man, hopefully Rev. Townsend, appeared in the door behind her. He wasn't very happy and started to scold us.

"Hey, what's going on here? What did you guys do to get my wife so upset! Go on! Move! Get out of here. You're not welcome around here!"

Hearing the commotion he had grabbed a baseball bat, just in case he might need it to deal with us.

Then his tone changed! He pointed at me, and asked his wife, "Could it really be him? Is that what has you so upset?"

"Yes!" she replied firmly. "That's Ira Fife Pointer. He's asking about his father!. Can't you tell? He looks so much like his father at that age!"

Rev. Townsend gave a huge sigh of relief, and noted that they had nothing to hide, so we had just as well come in. She settled down, and we entered not knowing what to do next. But we really had nothing to worry about, because after we had been seated, Rev. Townsend began.

"Yes, I knew your father. In fact, I was his best friend. I knew you too, young Ira, when your father brought you here in the summer of 1952 to preach a revival meeting for me."

I produced the picture, and asked if this was a picture of the two of us during that time, and he nodded yes.

"Then I'm puzzled!" I declared. "Did not my father get away from the Lord while in seminary, and did not my father and mother separate over that issue? And did not he virtually kidnap me from my mother just prior to coming to preach this revival for you? How could you invite him under those circumstances? He was away from the Lord (if he had ever been saved), and he brought a kidnapped son?"

"We didn't know the circumstances at that time. We thought he was still in seminary. I had invited him back in the Spring of 1952 as I graduated and left seminary to come here to pastor. We thought he had just brought you with him while your mother visited her family. We did not know he and your mother were separated, nor that he had taken you illegally from her."

"So where did he go when he left Joplin after the meeting with you? And have you heard from him since? He seems to have disappeared to everyone else!"

"Well," he explained, "during the meeting I could tell something was wrong. He was not the same powerful preacher of the past. So I asked him about it the last night of the services, after the final sermon. He smiled a sinister smile, and laughed a sinister laugh, as he noted gleefully that he had fooled me. It was then that he told me the above circumstances that you have mentioned.

"I asked him what he was going to do in the future, and he gave a clear but shocking answer. He planned to leave my home immediately (even that evening), and he informed me that I would never see him again. He was going to place you in a children's home where your mother could never find you, and that he was going to change his identity so completely that no one would ever be able to find him either. He planned to start all over again, without a wife and without a child. He said he eventually planned to get back into the ministry and make something of his life. But right now he was convinced that things were too mixed up, and he felt it was hopeless under the present circumstances (with an impending divorce and a deserted child) to ever advance in ministry. A broken marriage and a divorced wife and what would be considered to be a deserted child would shut every ministerial door for the future, especially the prestigious ones he hoped to enter."

"That sounds pretty selfish, doesn't it?" I commented, thinking out loud.

"It was!" he replied. "I tried to tell him that, but there was no reasoning with him. He was the most stubborn man I had ever met at this point. And what a shame. He was so brilliant and gifted. He had even written a book and gotten it published. He would have gone far in the ministry!"

"Did you ever hear from him after that?" I inquired.

"Well, your mother thought I had, and that I was not being honest with her. But with God as my witness today, I will tell you that I never heard from him again---not a letter, not a card, not a call, not a peep. And I was supposed to be his best friend. In all honesty again, not to hurt your feelings, I don't think your father had real friends, but was only friendly to people for his own selfish purposes. He used people and then burned the friendship or relationship, whether a supposed friend or relative!"

That was tough to hear---that your own father was a selfish scoundrel, even the one responsible for you growing up in a children's home. And now we seemed to be at another dead end! But, nonetheless, I wanted to make sure.

"So there is nothing you can tell me that might help me find him today?" I asked.

"Nothing solid! All I can say is this! If he stayed with the Evangelistic Baptist denomination, I would look for him at the top! He was not the kind of man to be satisfied working in obscurity. He wanted influence, prestige, position, and power, which only the top would bring him. Plus, he had the personality and drive to get there. If he is still alive, he's at the top. If he is dead, he either got there before dying, or he died trying to get there!"

I shuddered at the description of my father, but the few facts I did know about him seemed to back it up. He was a selfish, insensitive, self-centered ladder climber, who would discard or destroy any one who might stand in his way! I wondered why I wanted to find a father like that?

We stayed for supper that night with the Townsends at their insistence. No new information was forthcoming from our conversation. Then as we left to find a motel for the night, I kept thinking of Rev. Townsend's observation to look for him at the top! But even if I saw him, how would I know him. He would have a different name. He would look different after thirty years. He would also probably lie if ever confronted with his past. Besides, who was I to go around accosting denominational leaders or prominent pastors in such a manner, unless I was absolutely positive of an identity? Then Dink had a great idea.

"Preacha, if yer dad was bound and determined ta go ta da top, wouldn't he need some more education, say a doctor's degree? And wouldn't he have ta enroll in school wid his own name if he was wantin' ta transfer his previous college and seminary credit? But on da odder hand, if he did start all over wid a new identity, wouldn't he look a lot like dat old picture ya got? So, search da seminary and graduate school yearbooks!"

Maybe we weren't at a dead end---yet!

What Is an A-mil?

The next day as we flew home, we considered the last of our millennium views, the a-millennial position. Dink was still upset about what we had learned about my father, as was I, but he didn't seem to be able to set it aside.

"How in da world could a man treat a wife and kid like dat? A good wife an' a good kid, at dat! How could a guy be so amoral ta act dat way!?" he kept exclaiming.

I wanted to use his statement to introduce our subject.

"Hey, Dink, where did you get that word 'amoral?' Do you know what it means?" I poked at him.

"Sure, I ain't no dummy. I could even talk like ol' James and Samuel Seavers if I didn't have no scruples. An' dat's what dat word 'amoral' means. Its talkin' bout a guy widout any scruples---no morals."

"Then what would an a-millennialist believe?" I asked.

"Well, he'd be da guy dat don't believe in no millennium. Right? Amoral means a guy wid no moral principles. A-millennial means no millennium. See, I ain't no dummy."

"Dink, I never said you were, and you are right. The a-millennialist does not believe in an earthly millennium. Look at it like this."

The pre-mil believes in a literal earthly millennium
    with Christ reigning bodily on this earth.
The post mil believes in a literal earthly millennium
    without Christ reigning bodily on this earth.

> The a-mil rejects the idea of a literal earthly millennium
> but he does believe in the spiritual reign of Christ
> over this earth at the present time
> from His throne in heaven.

Then I listed this tenet of the a-mils with several others.

1. The a-mil believes the kingdom of Christ is a spiritual kingdom over which He, the victorious Christ of the cross, is now ruling from His throne in heaven by the power of His Word and the Holy Spirit.

2. The a-mil does not believe in a literal earthly kingdom of a literal one thousand years. Nor does the a-mil believe the spiritual kingdom is a literal one thousand year period.

3. The a-mil believes that Satan is now bound by the victory of Christ at the cross as described in the book of Revelation in chapter 20.

4. The a-mil believes that even though Christ has won the victory, and even though Satan is bound, there still exists a battle in this age between the kingdom of Christ and the kingdom of Satan.

5. The a-mil believes that the present age of battle between Christ and Satan will end with a form of tribulation and apostasy, and the appearance of a personal antichrist, and a time of the universal preaching of the gospel with many, including a great number of Jews being saved by Christ.

6. This spiritual kingdom of Christ, though it includes the great battle with Satan, and closes with the above described events, will ultimately end with the Second Coming of Christ followed by an immediate general judgment of all men.

7. The a-mil believes the general judgment will be followed immediately by the eternal state, with the saved entering into their eternal abode with Christ, and the lost condemned to their eternal abode of separation from God.

8. The a-mil view is usually associated with covenant theology, and therefore believes that God has one people throughout history, and one plan for that one people of God.

9. The a-mil position believes that the New Testament church is the new Israel, and many of the promises of God to His people in the Old Testament will be fulfilled in the New Covenant church.

I charted it in this manner:

```
            Christ Reigns        Christ Returns    A General
            from Heaven          at End of His     Judgment--
            During This Age      Spiritual Reign   Eternal State
                Λ                    V             for Saved
                Λ                    V             and Lost
         Christ's Resurrection    But no earthly
                Λ                  millennium---
                Λ                  only judgment as
    Christ Wins    The Battle with  Age Ends with
    the Victory    Satan Continues  Tribulation,
    at the Cross   on Earth         Apostasy and Antichrist
```

More will be said later about all the views, with an analysis of various Scripture passages. But for now this ended our general analysis of the positions..

Dink commented on the study, and then turned to the search once again.

"Preacha, what's da story of yer goin' inta dat orphanage? Who does dey say brought ya der? Surely some body checked ya inta dat place. Ain't dey got any records of yer admission, or da guy dat brought ya der?"

"Haven't I ever told you that story? Well, they tell me that I was brought in by a strange man, and before they could get the information, he slipped out. All he gave them was my name. I even wonder why he gave them that, unless it was pride in continuing the name of Ira Pointer. Maybe so, since he was having to give it up to begin a new identity."

"Well, couldn't yer mother have found ya, if he used dat name? It sure ain't no common name."

"My mother didn't have the resources, the time, nor the energy to pursue the matter. Her parents were sick. She had to bring in some money, so she developed the first nursing home. His family knew nothing. His friends knew nothing. She may have figured that he would not be so foolish as to use my name, if he was so determined to cut off his identity completely. I don't blame her for it. She was crushed and overwhelmed."

"Yeah, Preacha, I guess so. But I really wonder if he's gone to da top. If he has, I'll find him. I'm gonna ask every man at da top in da denomination if da name Ira Pointer means sumtin' ta him. I can tell by his reaction if he was at one time carryin' dat name!"

If you think he was kidding, you're wrong!!

The Pre-mil View of Revelation?

The days which followed were days of study for me, but also days of searching for my father with the help of Mack's people and Dink. Dink did search the top positions of our denominational institutions, just to see if Rev. Townsend might be correct. And though he found nothing, this new mystery seemed to help Dink in the loss of his son. I turned at this point to seek to understand how each of the millennial views handled the book of Revelation. I discovered the following.

The pre-millennialists are futurists. That is, they believe the greater portion of the book is still future, specifically, chapters 4-22.

The theonomic post-millennialists are preterists. That is, they believe that the greater part of Revelation was fulfilled at the time of the fall of Jerusalem in 70 AD. Obviously, then, the book of Revelation must have a much earlier date than many would give it---a date prior to 70 AD rather than a date in the 90's.

The a-millennialists are historicists. That is, they believe that the book of Revelation is a picture of the unfolding of history. Some see the same events unfolded several times to the reader in several parallel presentations of the same chronology of history.

Understanding that not all within each group agree in details on all matters, I decided I still needed to summarize the views in a chart form, and then give a more detailed outline of their convictions.

We might chart these positions as follows:

FUTURISTS

The Book of Revelation

Revelation 1-3	Revelation 4-22
The Past	The Future

PRETERISTS

The Book of Revelation

Revelation	Revelation
Chapters 1-20 (part)	Chapters 20 (part) to 22
The Past Judgement	The Beginning of the
of Jerusalem and Israel	Kingdom Which Extends
in 70 AD	to the Present and into the
	Future

HISTORICISTS

The Book of Revelation

The book of Revelation contains several movements which picture the history of the church in its entire history. Each movement covers the entire history of the church. Thus the book of Revelation is not a continuous single history of the church, but a book that gives us the entire picture of the history of the church through these several movements. Each movement pictures a different aspect or emphasis of the same full history of the church. (See a later chapter for a fuller presentation of this view.)

From this summary I went on to give a birds-eye view of the book of Revelation according to the pre-millennialist.

The Pre-mil View of the Book of Revelation

Revelation 1:19---A guideline for understanding the book
    John is commanded to write three things:
        the things which he has seen---chapter 1
        the things which are---chapters 2-3
        the things which shall be hereafter---chapters 4-22

I   THE THINGS WHICH JOHN HAS SEEN---Chp. 1
    Introduction 1:1-3
    Greeting---John is writing to the seven churches 1:4-9
    Vision---Jesus appearing to John on Patmos 1:9-18
    Command to write Revelation 1:19-20

II THE THINGS WHICH ARE Chps. 2-3
    A message to the seven churches in Asia
        Ephesus 2:1-7
        Smyrna 2:8-11
        Pergamos 2:12-17
        Thyatira 2:18-29
        Sardis 3:1-6
        Philadelpha 3:7-13

Laodicea   3:14-22
These are real literal churches of John's day with a real
   literal message for them in that hour from Christ.

III THE THINGS WHICH SHALL BE HEREAFTER
   Chps. 4-22
   A. The Heavenly Scene   Chps. 4-5
      1. John is called to heaven
      2. John sees things which must be hereafter
      3. John sees a throne in heaven
            One sat on the throne
            Twenty-four elders were around the throne
            Four living creatures around the throne
            Twenty four elders worship One on throne
            One on the throne is identified as Christ
            One on throne has a seven-sealed book
            Only the One on the throne is worthy
               to open the seals
            All at throne cry loudly, Worthy is the Lamb
   B. The Opening of the Seals   Chps. 6-11
      (The Tribulation Period Begins)
      1. Seal One--the Antichrist rides forth   6:1-2
      2. Seal Two--peace is taken from earth   6:3-4
      3. Seal Three--famine covers the earth   6:5-6
      4. Seal Four--death comes on earth   6:7-8
      5. Seal Five--souls of martyrs seen   6:9-11
      6. Seal Six--cataclysmic chaos   6:12-17
      Interval between sixth and seventh seals   7:1-17
         many saved during this tribulation period
      7. Seal Seven--Seven Trumpet Judgments
         (The Tribulation Period Continues)
         a. Trumpet 1--hail, fire and blood   8:7
         b. Trumpet 2--great mt. cast into sea   8:8-9

     c. Trumpet 3--great star from heaven 8:10-11

     d. Trumpet 4--sun, moon, stars smitten 8:11-13

     e. Trumpet 5--scorpion-like creatures 9:1-12

     f. Trumpet 6--army of horsemen sent 9:13-21

Interval between sixth and seventh trumpets

    Chps. 10:1-11:14

        Seven Thunder Judgments which John is

          told to seal up and write not 10:4

        Little Scroll which when eaten was sweet

          as honey but bitter to stomach 10:8-11

        Measuring of the Temple 11:1-2

        Two witness slain and raised 11:3-14

     g. Trumpet 7--Christ's rule comes 11:15-19

        Christ reigns forever as the kingdom of

          world becomes our Lord's kingdom

        Twenty-four elders worship Christ

C. The Identity of the Persons of Period Chps. 12-13

    (Information Needed for the Tribulation Period)

    1. Woman--Israel 12:1-2

    2. Dragon--Satan 12:3-4

    3. Man-child--Christ 12:5-6

    4. Satan cast from heaven 12:7-12

    5. Woman Israel persecuted by Satan 12:13-17

    6. Beast out of the sea 13:1-9

    7. Beast out of the earth 13:11-18

    Interval

        Lamb on Mt. Zion 14:1-5

        Doom of Babylon foretold 14:8

        Doom on beast's worshippers foretold 14:9-13

        Sharp sickle of judgment on earth 14:14-20

D. The Seven Last Plagues--Bowl Judgments Chp. 15

    (The Tribulation Period Continues)

Preparation 15:1-8
1. Bowl 1--sores on beast worshippers 16:1-2
2. Bowl 2--sea becomes blood 16:3
3. Bowl 3--rivers, etc. turn to blood 16:4-7
4. Bowl 4--sun scorches men with fire 16:8-9
5. Bowl 5---on throne of beast 16:10-11
     darkness
     gnawing of tongues for pain
     blasphemy of God;
     refusal to repent
6. Bowl 6--on great river Euphrates 16:12
7. Bowl 7--into the air 16:17-21
     great voice out of temple---it is done
     thunders and lightnings and great earthquake
     Babylon judged
     every island fled away
     mountains not found
     great hail upon men the weight of a talent
     men blaspheme God for the plague

E. The Doom of Babylon Chps. 17-18
many pre-millennialists
    believe this to be the judgment
      of the apostate church
      which has backed the Antichrist
        during this time

F. The Second Coming of Christ Chps. 19
1. Joy over destruction of Babylon 19:1-6
2. Joy at the marriage supper of Lamb 19:7-10
3. Judgment of the lost world at the Second Coming of JC 19:11-21
    a. the description of His coming 19:11-16
    b. the judgment at His coming 19:17-21

G. The Events after the Second Coming Chps. 20-22

1. The binding of Satan for 1000 years 20:1-2
2. The loosing of Satan after 1000 years 20:3
3. The first resurrection 20:4
4. The reign of Christ for 1000 years 20:4-6
5. The second resurrection 20:5-6
6. The work of Satan after 1000 years 20:7-8
   he is loosed out of prison
   he goes forth to deceive the nations
   he goes to make war against the saints
7. The judgment of Satan at this hour 20:9-10
   the fire of God comes down from heaven
   the followers of Satan are devoured
   Satan is cast into the lake of fire
   with the false prophet and beast
   where they are tormented day and night
   forever and ever
8. The Great White Throne judgement   20:11-15
   (Judgment of the Lost)
   a. The Judge--Christ
   b. The Judging--from the book and books
   c. The Judged--the dead small and great
   d. The Judgement--those not in book of life
      were cast into the lake of fire
9. The new heavens and new earth 21:1-22:5
10. The final message of the book 22:6-21

As I was deeply involved in this extended outline of Revelation according to the pre-mils, a phone call came. With some indifference to whomever might be calling, I picked up the phone, and spoke a rather nonchalant hello. But it was not an indifferent message which greeted me.

"Ira F. Pointer?" the voice asked. "I understand you are looking for me?"

My ears perked up. I wasn't aware that I was looking for anyone but my father?

"And who are you, sir, that I would be looking for you?" I asked with growing interest.

"I'm Ira F. Pointer!" came the flooring reply.

"Can you prove that?" I asked suspiciously.

"If you'll give me a chance, I can and will!" he replied.

"Where are you now?" I queried with deepest interest.

"I'm downtown at the bus station in your town."

"How will I recognize you?" I asked, seeking to pin him down.

"I'll be the one with the black cap and glasses, along with a brown coat and blue suitcase!" he replied curtly.

"I'll be there in five minutes!" I shot back. "Just stay there!"

"Don't worry! I didn't come all the way from California to dodge you. I'll be waiting."

It appeared that I was about to have some kind of a revelation very soon---though not a Biblical one. Nor was I sure it was even a true one.

Where Is Your Proof?

As I drove to the bus station, I went by Dink's house, and picked him up. I wanted his sharp discernment of this situation, just so my emotions wouldn't get carried away. As we drove he summed up my thoughts.

"Where'd dis guy come from, Preacha? Who told him we was lookin fer him? An why all of a sudden, he wants ta see ya, when he was gone all dose years! It sounds fishy ta me, Preacha."

I agreed with him, and shut down the conversation as we pulled into the bus station area. Sure enough, there standing on the corner was a man in a black cap and glasses, with a blue suitcase and brown coat.

As I stepped out of the car, I gathered my emotions. Could this really be my father---the man who had kidnapped me from my mother and put me in the children's home years ago?

He recognized me as I walked toward him, and his eyes looked me over with apparent deep interest.

"Are you the one claiming to be Ira Pointer?" I began.

"Yes, and are you the one claiming to be my son?" he countered.

I didn't like his attitude nor his statement of the matter, as it was not my identity which stood in question. And I had not claimed to be his son, unless he really was Ira Pointer. Nonetheless I nodded, and suggested that we get in the car and go to a restaurant and talk. He agreed, and there was mostly silence, till we arrived at the restaurant, and were seated.

"What proof do you have that you are Ira Pointer, my father!" I challenged him. "Please forgive my directness or what may appear to be a sharpness, but surely you understand my feelings after all these years and in light of your past actions, if you are Ira Pointer." I argued.

He nodded his understanding, and apologized for maybe getting off to a bad start. He acknowledged that perhaps his approach was too direct, lacking tact and understanding of my feelings.

"Well, son, I'm not sure how to answer your question of proof. I think I can give it to you in time, but I don't have any document to show you my claim. I have spent the last thirty years erasing all the evidence that would give you the proof you would seek. Now what can I say or give you to prove my claim? Only information? So ask any questions you want, about you, your mother, my existence since putting you in the children's home, etc."

"Well, for starters, begin with how you knew I was looking for you, how you knew where to find me, and why you decided to come forward now?"

"Well, I learned you were looking for me, and where I could find you from Rev. Townsend and his wife. You may not believe me, but I have been thinking about trying to find you for a long time. I've carried a lot of guilt over the years, and I hope you understand how I want to make things right now, if that's possible. Can you imagine my surprise when I called Rev. Townsend the other evening for the first time in thirty years, and he told me of your visit with him? And that you were looking for me? I wonder if this is God's providence putting together a reunion between us all."

"Us all?" I asked.

"Yes, I would like to see your mother also, but I know she will not see me, unless you might intercede for me!" he offered, seemingly with honesty.

"Well, there will be a lot of discussion before we can do that. There will have to be certainty of your claim before I would ever be any kind of an advocate for you. And even then, she may not see you, even if I ask her to."

"But you must be tired after riding the bus from California!" I offered. "Let's get you a motel room, and give you some time to rest, and we'll pick you back up for supper."

I had no idea if he had money to pay for it, but it was evident that any determination of his claim was going to take a few days.

He agreed, and soon he was settled and Dink and I were driving back to the church.

"What do you make of that, Dink?" I asked, knowing I would get an honest answer.

"I say again that der's sumptin fishy bout dat guy! He ain't da real thing!" he replied.

"Why do you say that?" I asked.

"Well, too many tings jus' don't square. He don't look like dat picture! His timing is jus' too coincidental! He's shifty in his talk! He don't look like no straight shooter in his eyes. He's gotta smart-aleck attitude!"

"But how did he know Rev. Townsend?" I asked again.

"I dunno! But he's da first guy I'd call, if I was you, Preacha! You can call him from my house!" he offered.

"Why not? There's no better time than the present!"

The A-mil Preterist View of Revelation?

When I let Dink off at his house, I also called Rev. Townsend. He confirmed that someone had called and had said he was Ira Pointer, but on the phone and after these many years, he could not guarantee that this was the man's true identity. He couldn't recognize the voice for certain. He noted that the man knew a lot about the past history of Ira Pointer, and even of the events of their past relationship. He seemed to think this was the real Ira Pointer, but could not be sure of it.

I also called Mack Turnover, since he had mentioned a man in California, who had claimed to be my father. Could this be the same guy, as my present visitor? After a few moments, he assured me it wasn't possible, since the man of whom he spoke was now in jail.

Thus when we got off the phone, we agreed we had learned nothing. We still had a man with a claim that he could not prove and which we could not disprove. We decided that we would interview (Dink used the word interrogate) him that evening at supper.

In the meantime, I had a few hours until our supper meeting, so I decided to turn my thoughts, as best I could, back to the book of Revelation. Having given a birds-eye view of the book according to the pre-millennialist, I decided to tackle a summary of one of the a-mill views. Part of the problem was which a-mil view to present. I decided that it would be the <u>a-mil preterist view</u>. I had come across a book that gave an excellent summary of that position.[1]

I reminded myself that the preterist view saw most of the book of Revelation fulfilled at the time of the fall of Jerusalem in 70 AD, and that the a-mil position believed in a spiritual millennium and not a literal one.

I noted again that the author of this book stated the following concerning his position

1. That this view (the a-mil preterist view) stated that the first nineteen chapters of Revelation and part of the twentieth chapter had already been fulfilled.

2. That the book of Revelation is a message of encouragement and exhortation to the churches in Asia Minor in the first century in light of the impending persecutions to come upon them.

3. That the book of Revelation concerns primarily the fall of the apostate Jewish commonwealth and its religious system and the defeat of the last world kingdom (the Roman kingdom). These were the two great foes of the church of that day.

4. That the book of Revelation concerns also the story of the unavenged martyrs, who are mentioned numerous times in the unfolding of the book of Revelation.

Daniel 7:21-22,	Revelation 2:13
Revelation 6:9-11	Revelation 7:13-17
Revelation 10:6-7	Revelation 12:11
Revelation 13:7-10	Revelation 14:12-13

Revelation 16:5-7   Revelation 17:6
Revelation 18:20-24 Revelation 19:2-3
Revelation 20:4

5. That the great emphasis on these unavenged martyrs, plus the several verses which speak of the events of Revelation coming to pass soon (see list below), indicate a more immediate fulfillment of the events mentioned in the book, rather than a later fulfillment as seen by pre-mils and other views.

Revelation 1:1
   things which must shortly come to pass
Revelation 1:3
   the time is at hand
Revelation 22:6
   things which must shortly come to pass
Revelation 22:10
   the time is at hand

With those introductory notations, I began a brief outline of the book.

Revelation 1:19---The Divinely-stated outline of the book
   John is commanded to write from his perspective
      things of the past---Revelation 1
      things of the present---Revelation 2-3
      things of the future---Revelation 4-22

I   SECTION ONE---Chapters 4-12
   Chapters 4-5
      This is a statement of God's care for His suffering saints, as John is taken into the heavenly throne

room, in the hour that God's judgment (the fall of Jerusalem in 70 AD) is about to begin. John is given a reassuring glimpse of God's divine control and care.

Chapters 6-11

These chapters tell us of the events preceding the fall of Jerusalem in 70 AD.

The breaking of the seals of judgment
> Seals 1-4
>> Conquest, War, Famine, Death
>>> (See Luke 21:9-11---these things will precede the destruction of Jerusalem)
> Seal 5
>> The plight of Christ's martyred saints of that day---their case is deferred for later judgment
> Seal 6
>> The judgment to come upon the Jewish persecutors at the time of the siege and fall of the city of Jerusalem in 70 AD (see 6:12-17)
>> The preservation of a great number of Jewish saints during the siege of Jersusalem which is to come in 70 AD (see 7:4-8)
>> The great multitude of Gentile believers who will soon die for their faith also (see 7:9-17)
> Seal 7
>> This seal takes place prior to the fall of Jerusalem.

This seal opens with a half-hour's silence---
the calm before the storm of judgment

This seal brings the fullness of God's judgment upon the earth through the seven
trumpet judgments as the prayers of the
saints have been heard (see 8:3-5)

The first four plagues (see chapter 8) pertain to God's judgment poured out
through nature---an indirect judgment---
predicting the several years of ravage
and pillage prior to the destruction of
Jerusalem itself

The next two plagues (see chapter 9) pertain
to the coming judgment upon man---
direct judgment, also referring to the
coming destruction of Jerusalem

There is a brief announcement in Chapter 10
which concerns another prophecy yet to
be given

The early part of chapter 11 speaks of the
presence of two witnesses who will be
sent of God to Jerusalem prior to the fall
of Jerusalem in 70 AD

Chapter 12 is a transitional chapter which
carries the reader from Jerusalem to Rome.
The transition is accomplished by moving
back to the beginning to the very roots of
Christianity to sketch the movement up to
the present day of the writer of the book of
Revelation. Within the story of the historical
development of Christianity, we see clearly
the following: the Hebrew environment into
which the church was born; the gradual

development of the church into a world-wide entity; the birth of the Messiah to the woman, the Old Testament Church; the story of Satan's attempt to destroy the Messiah through the unbelieving Jews; Satan's attack upon the church when it becomes clear he cannot destroy the Messiah; God's protection of His own, rescuing them from the fierce attack upon Jerusalem; the casting of the devil to the earth because of his defeat at Calvary; the devil's lashing out in fury knowing his time is short. With this the transition is complete, as Satan's wrath moves to being poured out against Christ's church through the Roman government.

At this point, I was interrupted by Dink. It was almost 6:00 PM and we needed to pick up the professed Ira Pointer. Section two of the a-mil preterist view of Revelation 13-22 would have to wait until tomorrow!

As we made our way to the motel, we discussed what might be our approach to the encounter we were facing. We had a few ideas, but I decided that our dependence was upon the Lord. He would have to guide us, and in some way at sometime reveal to us the truth.

---

[1]Jay Edward Adams, *I Will Tell Thee the Mystery* (Walker, Iowa: Perspective Press, 1965).

What Should I Believe?

Our guest was waiting for us when we arrived at the motel---a good sign for the moment, that he had some sense of responsibility and dependability. After ordering our food at a local restaurant, I began my questions.

"Have you thought of any way you can prove your claim that you are my father, Ira Pointer?" I began.

"Did you call Rev. Townsend?" he inquired.

"Yes, and he said you knew much about Ira Pointer and his background, but that he could not guarantee your claimed identity either by voice or by information you gave him!" I replied. "Have you got any other ideas?"

"No, as I said before, I spent thirty years getting rid of all the evidence, and now that I need it, I either don't have any or cannot resurrect any."

"Well, then, tell me where have you been these thirty years? Maybe that will open some door whereby we can determine your claim!" I suggested.

He agreed, and then told me that when he left Rev. Townsend's that summer thirty years ago, that he brought me to the children's home. He did know the name and location of the home, and the date I had been placed there. He said he even remembered the name of the administrator that he talked with when he left me---a Mr. Farnsworth. From there he went to California and spent a few years re-establishing his identity. He changed his name, illegally, and got all the papers he needed, again illegally, and spent those few years there building a history so he could make his next move.

When I asked what his next move was, he told us that he came back to Seminary City, enrolled in school there, and finished the bachelor and master degrees. He even pastored several churches in the process, and then worked on a doctorate. Obviously, I asked for the names of those churches, which he gave me readily without batting an eye.

Next, when he had finished his doctorate, he taught in a Bible school in Texas, and, without my requesting it, he supplied the name of that institution as well. Then he moved to teach at a seminary in California where he had been for the remainder of his lost years.

Then I did have some questions.

"What name did you use all these years?"

"I took the name of Samuel Barwell, which I am still using today," he replied.

"Did you ever get married, and have children?" I further inquired.

"No, to be honest, I never got over your mother! She was one of a kind, never to be replaced. Over the years I came to realize what a fool I had been to treat her as I did, whereby I lost her, to say nothing of my deep sorrow for what I did to you. I thought of seeking reconciliation with her at times. But I guess I was too stubborn or proud or fearful of her further rejection, or something. Maybe I was fearful of how it would ruin my present life as a professor in a highly respected school. I just never could force myself to contact her. I fell into a pattern of total consumption with my work in teaching and preaching. It wasn't until just last week that I finally surrendered to the growing conviction that I had to seek to deal with this matter---not only with your mother, but also with you."

With this, he began to cry. He was either a skilled and compulsive liar, or he had to be telling the truth. I looked at Dink for a second, and he rolled his eyes at me, seeming to give a sign that he did not believe his story. I was at a dead end again as to what I could do next to substantiate his story. Even if it all checked out, which it did as we investigated it in the next few days, how was I to know that he was my father? But then again, what motive would he have to claim my father's identity other than a true desire for reconciliation?

I was really shocked when he grabbed the check and paid the bill at the restaurant, even adding, "I hope you don't think I have come to mooch off of you for food or even the motel. Believe me, I am well able to take care of my bills and expenses."

My only question then was why he had rode a bus all the way from California, instead of flying. He countered that he was fearful of planes and air travel.

We dropped our guest at the motel, and as soon as he was out of the car, Dink gave his opinion.

"I jus' don't like it! It jus' ain't right. I don't know dat guy's motive and goal, but he ain't yer father!"

At this point I did not know what to believe! So we had Mack investigate the schools and his claims concerning them. It all checked out, in that a Samuel Barwell had attended school in Seminary City, and had taught in Texas and California.

But one thing was still suspicious. Samuel Barwell no longer taught at either of the schools he had mentioned. When I asked him later, if he was still teaching in California, he said no. That seemed to be a contradiction to his earlier statement that day.

The A-mil Preterist View
of Revelation (cont.)?

Terry and I stayed awake long into the night discussing the meeting with Samuel Barwell, or Ira Pointer, or whoever he was. We decided that she needed to meet him, as I trusted her discernment in such matters as well.

The next morning I called him, and made arrangements for him to come to our home for lunch. He sounded excited to be able to meet my wife and my son---his grandson, he noted.

So since I had my sermon preparation finished for the next Sunday, I gave myself once again to the study before me on eschatology. I needed to finish the a-mil preterist view of the book of Revelation, but first I reviewed the first section, Chapters 1-12.

The A-mil Preterist View

I noted the following concerning this interpretation of the book of Revelation in Chapters 1-12:

1. This view believes the first nineteen chapters and part of chapter twenty had already been fulfilled.

2. This view believes Revelation is a message of encouragement to the people of the writer's day.

3. This view believes the book was concerned with the fall of the Jewish religious system and of the last world kingdom of Rome, the two great foes of the church of that day.

4. This view believes the book also was concerned with the story of the unavenged martyrs who are mentioned numerous times in the book of Revelation.

5. This view believes that the majority of the events in the book of Revelation would come to pass soon (soon from the writer John's perspective), in light of several phrases in the book.

6. In Section One or Chapters 4-12, which we had already covered, we are shown events which precede the fall of Jerusalem in 70 AD.

Then I made the following notes in outline form to cover the final chapters of the book of Revelation according to the position known as the a-mil preterist view.

II SECTION TWO---Chapters 13-19
   Chapter 13
        The first beast---see chapter 17:7-18 where this symbol is clearly identified. The beast in Revelation 17 is the same as the first beast of chapter 13, and the beast is imperial Rome, while the woman of chapter 17 is the city of Rome.
        The second beast is a religious man or a religious movement that empowers the first beast.

Both of these pertain to the establishment of the Roman empire of the writer's day.

Chapter 14

The believing Jews to be saved at the time of the fall of Jerusalem are mentioned again.

The visions of the six angels and the Savior introduces the reader to the characters, forces and themes of prophecy which follow---the preaching of the gospel, the fall of Rome and the judgments of God.

Chapter 15-16

The bowls in this chapter are bowls of wrath which have been filling up for years against Rome. They are now full and ready to be poured out on the earth.

The bowls of judgment are now poured out upon Rome. The first four bowls describe the judgments on the empire of Rome as a whole. The sixth bowl is poured out on the city of Rome itself---the seat of the beast and the empire. This is the smashing and breaking of the image by the kingdom of God as seen by Daniel.

The battle mentioned at the end of chapter 16 is not the second coming of Christ, but the battle with the beast (the Roman Empire present in John's day). This is the same event as seen at the end of Revelation 19.

Chapter 17

This chapter gives an explanation and interpretation of the primary symbols. John says in verse seven that he is going to give the identity of the woman and the beast. In verses 8-16 he makes it clear that the beast is Rome, and in verse 18 he identifies the woman as the city of Rome itself. The terms leave no doubt as to the identification of these two symbols. All knew in John's day, and all know now, that Rome was built on seven hills.

Chapter 18

This chapter is a song of victory, celebrating the fall of the city of Rome. The a-mil preterist view would acknowledge that the fall of Rome did not take place as suddenly as this chapter seems to indicate. It was actually years before Rome fell. But this is similar to the prophecies of the OT concerning the fall of literal Babylon (see Jeremiah 51:8), which speak of it as done prior to its actually happening.

Chapter 19

This chapter begins with the marriage supper of Christ and His bride. Then verses 11-21 speak of the establishment of the kingdom of God, which Daniel promised would supplant the four world kingdoms, the final one being the kingdom of the Roman Empire. This section is not the second coming of Christ. This is the destruction of the world empire by the Word of God, and the establishment of the spiritual world-wide kingdom of God (Christ reigning in heaven). This is not to deny the second coming of Christ, but to argue that this section of Scripture is not referring to the second coming. This is the battle previously spoken of in Revelation 16:14-16. The Savior came to rule all the nations as King of Kings and Lord of Lords at the death and resurrection and exaltation of

Christ. This is the coming promised in Matthew 16:28, as Christ promised that some of those standing there would not see death, till they saw the Son of man coming in His kingdom. This reign of Christ which was grounded in His death, and resurrection, and exaltation, began the final overthrow of the fourth world kingdom.

Chapter 20

This chapter begins where chapter 19 ends. Having dealt with the defeat of the two enemies of the church, we are now given the details of the end of Satan's war against God. When the King of Kings began to reign over the nations, we are told that Satan's time would be short (12:12). Satan is seized and cast into the abyss, and the new era begins. The kingdom of God began with the death of Christ (a spiritual kingdom), but then it was fully realized when the Roman empire fell. The period that Satan's crumbling world-kingdom existed alongside the new world-kingdom of God was the "short time" spoken of in Revelation. Thus the 1000 year period (a symbolic number) began in the New Testament times and continues to the present. Also, this is the period when Satan is bound, which does not mean that all his activity is stopped, for Christ indicated that the strong man had been bound (Matthew 12:29). The word bind can be used and yet not mean a total restriction. The context of this chapter indicates the meaning of the binding, when it says "that he should deceive the nations (Gentiles) no more until the thousand years should be fulfilled." (Revelation 20:3). As the author, who was mentioned above, says,

This partial binding is now in effect. From the beginning of pagan world-empire, until New Testament times, the gentiles as a whole were under the sway of the deceptive prince of darkness. Who will deny his sway has been shattered? Who will deny that the gospel has now spread to many lands and peoples? Who will deny that the great task of missions which the Savior set before his church after his ascension was identical with this purpose of freeing the gentiles from the deception of Satan. Who will deny that the means by which the missionary endeavour is to be carried out is the Word of God (as shown in Revelation 19)?[1]

This same author continues:

Satan is not allowed to reestablish his fallen world dominion until the thousand years are finished. What believer will deny that ever since the fall of Rome, there has been only one truly world-wide kingdom in existence--the kingdom of God?[2]

The text in Revelation 20 continues telling us that at end of the period during which Satan is bound, he is released from his binding, and returns to his old ways, as he goes out to deceive the Gentile nations once again. This is the period described in II Thessalonians 2, and by our Savior as the time it will be impossible to find faith on the earth. This may also be a time when many Jews turn to faith in Christ, as Romans 11 seems to indicate. Satan at this time gathers the nations against the saints in a last attempt to destroy the kingdom of God and restore his lost world kingdom. But Christ returns in flaming fire and destroys both him and his army. Here in chapter 20 is the Second Coming of Christ. It follows the spiritual millennium which is now upon the earth, and it precedes the final judgment of God.

Another issue concerns the meaning of the first resurrection. It is not the new birth, because these martyrs were regenerated long before the time of their martyrdom, and therefore could not be said to "live" in that sense after death.[3] Neither does "live" mean going to heaven. The term "living" speaks of that which is given to the martyrs which other Christians do not receive until the thousand years have past. But also, one must realize, that according to this interpretation, the phrase "rest of the dead" refers not to the unsaved dead, but to all other non-martyred Christians. Thus the martyrs receive something special. But what is it? Context must tell us. Revelation 20:2 tells us that they are to become priests of God and they are to live and reign with Christ. Thus the living spoken of in this context in reference to the first resurrection is to become a priest and king with Christ in all of the fullness of those terms. This is a special heavenly reign with Christ only for these martyrs at this time. The rest of the dead believers will receive this blessing at the close of Christ's spiritual reign. These martyrs receive this blessing immediately upon their death. To live means these martyrs begin to participate with Christ immediately in the activities in which He is now engaged.

The rest of the dead are termed as living after the spiritual reign of Christ. This cannot be the lost or unsaved dead, due to the fact that their resurrection is not unto life but unto death. These (the rest of the dead) are resurrected to life not death. Thus the first resurrection includes the martyrs of verse four and the "rest of the dead" of verse five. It is the second death which speaks of the unsaved. Those who are not found in the Lamb's book of life will experience the second death, as they are cast into the lake of fire (Revelation 20:6, 14-15).

From these considerations comes the realization that Revelation 20:11-15 (generally known as the Great White Throne Judgment) is the final judgment of all men, not just a judgment of unbelievers.

Chapters 21-22
The redemption of the physical earth is reserved till the last. To quote the author and work mentioned above:

Just how literally the concepts contained in these chapters are to be taken is difficult to say. Undoubtedly, there is both figurative and non-figurative language side-by-side, as in the rest of the Apocalypse. The main thrust of the passage, if taken literally would seem to indicate that believers after the judgment will dwell upon the renewed earth. This fits the glorified state far better than the semi-golden, sinful premillennial millennium. This condition, with the new Jerusalem descending to the new earth, will be literally, "heaven on earth."....All this---if the chapters are to be understood literally.

However, a literal interpretation involves the idea of God dwelling literally upon the earth in some *special* way (cf. Revelation 21:2, 22, 23; 22:3). This last idea seems somewhat unlikely when understood literally. Yet, we know that God [the word God is left out in the writer's quote, and it seems to be a typo, so we have inserted it] is capable of manifesting Himself in the Shekinah glory. It is wise to reserve judgment about the exact location of the eternal abode of the believer. These chapters may be attempts to express the humanly-inexpressible glory of the blessings which await Christ's own.[4]

I gave a sigh of relief when I finished these notes. But then I noted that I had better hurry. I wanted to be at the house when Samuel Barwell arrived!

---

[1]Jay Edward Adams, *I Will Tell Thee the Mystery* (Walker, Iowa: Perspective Press, 1965), p. 79

[2]Ibid.

[3]Ibid., pp. 84-85. Many a-mils see the first resurrection to be regeneration.

[4]Ibid., p. 88.

The Post-mil Preterist View
of Revelation?

I arrived home just a few minutes before Mr. Barwell appeared at the door. As he did, he looked a lot different than the previous day. He was in a suit with a freshly pressed shirt, and he sported a sharp looking necktie. He looked much different than from the first time I had seen him yesterday, but I guess anyone who has ridden cross-country in a bus will look a little worn and bedraggled. He now resembled a professor.

Our son, Ira, Jr., who was nine years old by now, was in school, and that was probably best in light of the uncertainty of our visitor's claim. It did not take us long to get at the heart of the matter before us.

I began by asking, "Is there no way we can be certain of your identity and claim?"

This was before the use of DNA to determine paternity. Other methods, such as blood testing, were really not very accurate. Birth certificates had no finger prints in those days as some did by the 1980's. So I was searching for some means for a clear and undeniable manner to substantiate his claim.

His answer was a little premature, but seemed to have been a great deal of his motive for even coming.

"There is probably only one person who could positively identify me, and that is your mother! Surely, regardless of how much I have changed in appearance, she could identify me by characteristics of speech or actions, or even by information that we shared together. That is the only way of verification that I can imagine!"

"Do you really think that is possible---that she would see you and talk to you?" I asked skeptically.

"Maybe not for my sake, but perhaps for your sake!" he answered.

"Do you really want to tear open the wounds of her heart after all these years? Who do you think you are to have treated her in such a manner, walking out on her when you wished, taking her only child, to be gone for thirty years, and then you want to waltz back into her life on your terms as far as time and reason---because you've decided you want to rebuild the relationship? Is that not rather arrogant and self-centered?"

"Would you believe it if I told you that I would just like to see her, to ask for her forgiveness, and that I would walk away immediately if she told me to do so?" he asked. Would you believe me if I told you that I would be blessed if all that came of this was our restoration---yours and mine, as father and son?" he continued.

I saw tears in his eyes once again. I thought, "Boy, this guy is good, if he's not for real!"

Before he left, I admonished him not to contact my mother, but to leave it up to me. I was not sure how I would do it, or what I would say, but she was the only one, so it seemed, who could solve the puzzle.

When he was gone, I asked Terry what she thought. She was convinced that he was probably my father. Yet she admitted that positive proof was going to be difficult--- unless we could get my mother to cooperate in identifying him.

Thus, it seemed inevitable that there had to be a confrontation between them, if we were ever going to get to the bottom of this mystery.

After further discussion with Terry, I made my way back to the church to pursue the other passion of my heart. I decided that I would next summarize the <u>post-mil preterist view</u> of the book of Revelation. I didn't know how far I would get, but I could at least get started.

The Post-mil Preterist View of Revelation

I reminded myself that the preterist view believed that most of the book of Revelation (up to and into part of chapter 20) had already been fulfilled prior to the fall of Jerusalem in 70 AD. I marveled that one could hold a preterist view under either the a-mil structure of prophecy or the post-mil framework of eschatology. I was anxious to see how they might differ.

Some preliminary ideas (not distinct from the a-mil preterist) were noted:[1]

1. The book is written to the churches of John's day, with a special message for them. Thus any interpretation of the book must take this into account, and cannot immediately jump into our day for its fulfillment, while ignoring the state and conditions of the early believers of the first century church.

2. The book states that the prophecy contained therein will shortly come to pass, or that these events are at hand (see Revelation 1:1, 3, 19 and Revelation 22:6,

7, 12, 20). Thus, again one must not carry them off into the future for their fulfillment, while ignoring these clear statements of a "soon" fulfillment.

3. If the above is true, then the book of Revelation was written before 70 AD and not sometime in the nineties as has been the traditional date.

4. The theme of the book of Revelation is 1:7, which states that Christ is coming with the clouds, and every eye shall see him, even those who pierced Him; and all the tribes of the earth will mourn over Him. The preterist view believes that this coming is not the Second Coming, but the coming of Christ to judge Israel at the siege of Jerusalem in 70 AD. The reason for this belief is that this coming will be witnessed by those who pierced Christ, which cannot be said of those on earth at His Second Coming. It is an historical fact that thousands of Jews perished at the destruction of the city of Jerusalem.

I   REVELATION 1-5---Preparation for Judgment

   A. Christ as the defender of His people   1:12ff
   B. Christ as the messenger to His people   2-3
   C. God as Sovereign on the throne of judgment   4
   D. Christ as the Judge of Israel   5
         the seven-sealed scroll
               is God's divorce decree against Israel

II REVELATION 6-19---Judgement of Israel at the time of the Fall of Jerusalem

   A. The First Six Seals of Judgment

      1. <u>Seal One</u>---pictures the Roman army coming victoriously against Israel and Jerusalem
      2. <u>Seal Two</u>---pictures the devastation of the Jewish civil war
      3. <u>Seal Three</u>---pictures famine which will plague Israel at this time
      4. <u>Seal Four</u>---pictures the dead of Israel at this horrible time of Jerusalem's destruction
      5. <u>Seal Five</u>---the martyrs gathered around the altar of heaven crying for vindication picture the Christian martyrs of this time
      6.. <u>Seal Six</u>---the phenomena picture the stark collapse of Israel's government at the fall of Jerusalem

   B. The First Interlude
      1. The temporary halt of judgment
      2. The 144,000 sealed saints are a picture of Jewish converts to Christianity who live in Jerusalem who are protected by God at the time of the fall of Jerusalem

   C. The Seventh Seal or the Seven Trumpets (seventh seal opens seven trumpet judgments)
      1. Trumpets 1-4---Judgment on Things
      2. Trumpets 5-7---Judgment on Men
         a. <u>Fifth Trumpet</u>
            demonic torment for five months at the siege of Jerusalem
         b. <u>Sixth Trumpet</u>
            Roman reinforcements sent to Jerusalem

D. The Second Interlude (10:1-11)
>> Christ stands straddling land and sea
>> declaring that Israel's time is up

E. The Measuring of the Temple   (Ch 11)
>> John is told to measure the temple
>>> in the holy city---where Christ was killed
>>> (the measuring is for judgment)

F. The Protection of God's Witnesses   (Ch 11)
>> During the time of the siege of 42 months
>>> two prophets (maybe symbolic of a
>>>> small group of believers) who
>>>> remained in Jerusalem during the
>>>> siege appear to testify against it

G. The Protection of the Jerusalem Church (Ch 12)
>> This is a flashback to the early church in the
>>> city of Jerusalem, as it is being protected
>>> from the persecution of Satan.
>> This covers the time from Christ's ministry
>>> through the book of Acts and up until the
>>> destruction of Jerusalem.

H. The Two Beasts   (Ch 13)
> 1. The First Beast
>> Generically the Beast is Rome
>> Specifically the Beast is Nero Caesar---
>>> the Roman emperor of his day
>>>> who persecuted Christians
>>>> for a period of 42 months
>>>> prior to the fall of Jerusalem

> 2. The Second Beast
>> This beast rises from Palestine and
>>> backs and energizes the authority
>>> of the First Beast

    I.   The Destruction of Babylon   (Ch 14)
        1. Babylon stands for the city of Jerusalem
        2. Jerusalem and Israel are ripe for judgment
        3. Blood flows as the battle rages between the
            Romans and the Jews
    J. · The Seven Vials of Wrath   (Ch 15)
           this is a picture of the final assault
           upon Jerusalem
    K. The Final Defeat of Jerusalem   (Chs 17-19)
           the woman (Jerusalem) who is
               so arrogant and proud
               so full of sin
               is judged by God as Rome defeats her
                   at the fall of the city of Jerusalem
           the coming in Revelation 19
               is not Christ's final coming
               but His coming to judge Jerusalem
                   in 70 AD
    L. The Bride of Christ   (Chs 20-22)
        (we move beyond the destruction of Jerusalem)
           a.   Christ rules from heaven
               with His saints
                over the earth
               in Revelation 20:1-6
               for 1000 years (symbolic figure)
           b.   Satan is bound during this time
               it is a spiritual not a literal binding
               it does not result in total inability
                   or total inactivity by Satan
               it began in the first century
                   during the ministry of Christ
                   secured legally at His
                       death and resurrection

it is evidenced by the fall of Judaism
  the church's first foe
it is made clear by Jerusalem's fall
it continues through the Christian era
it is evidenced by the gospel's power
  to the Gentiles
    who were under Satan's power
c. The two resurrections---first and second
  the first resurrection
    speaks of salvation as it is
      the spiritual resurrection
        of believers
    this leads
      to the saints enthronement
      with Christ
      during His spiritual reign
  the second resurrection
    is the resurrection of the lost
      to judgment
    at the end of the reign of Christ
    to be cast into the lake of fire
d. The loosing of Satan
  Satan is loosed from his binding
    for a little while
    at the end of Christ's reign
    to gather a group of rebels
      to war against God
  but fire comes down from God
    out of heaven
    to devour them
    while Satan is cast into the lake
      of fire

e. THIS IS ALSO THE HOUR
OF CHRIST'S SECOND COMING
IN POWER AND GREAT GLORY
AS HE CASTS ALL EVIL INTO
ETERNAL JUDGMENT

f. The new creation or new Jerusalem
this began in the first century
though it stretches into eternity
in its final consummation
it is the fullness of His reign and rule
it is now for eternity
it expresses the glory of our salvation
it contains His bride---the Church

CONCLUDING CHALLENGES ---Revelation 22:6ff
1. These prophecies are true
2. These prophecies are near
3. These prophecies are for the early hearers
4. These prophecies must be received

I noted several other observations before I closed my time of study.

1. This was just one presentation of a post-mil preterist view. Though others of this same conviction might disagree in some way, there would be agreement on the total framework and idea that most of the book of Revelation was fulfilled before the fall of Jerusalem.

2. There would be some agreement between the a-mil preterist and the post-mil preterist, even though it must be noted that some of the details are different.

3. The real message and emphasis of the post-mil view in the presentation, which emphasizes a powerful and growing kingdom of Christ, is not until one comes to the last three chapters of the book of Revelation. This growing kingdom would have begun with the fall of Jerusalem, and is continuing until today and even into the future.

About this time the phone rang, and it was Mr. Barwell.

"I called your mother, and she said she didn't want to see me!" he said with some seeming sadness.

I was not happy with his end run.

"I thought we had decided that I would call her?" I shot back trying to throttle my impatience.

"Yes, I guess we did, but I thought maybe she would listen to me after all these years!" he whined excusingly.

I didn't feel like arguing with him, so I told him we would talk about it the next day. I also needed some time to think as to our next move.

Little did I know what would transpire by the next morning!

------

[1]The author must admit a bit of an anachronism in this chapter as this outline of the post-mil preterist view is that taken from a book by Kenneth L. Gentry, Jr., *He Shall Have Dominion* (Tyler, Texas: Institute for Christian Economics, Second Edition, Revised, 1997). The setting of the story before us is the fall of 1982, while the first edition of this book is 1992. That is the "anachronism" of which we speak. For one wishing to know more of the post-mil preterist view, the best and clearest writings on the subject today have been done by Dr. Gentry (see the bibliography at the end of this work).

Will the Real Ira Pointer Please Stand Up?

The next morning as I went by the motel to have breakfast with Mr. Barwell (I couldn't bring myself to call him by a fatherly name until the matter was settled), I was shocked to learn that he had checked out just a few hours ago. The only place I knew to look for him was at the bus station.

I found him over in a corner reading as if nothing had happened. He didn't seem to mind when I came walking up, but I think I rattled him when I spoke.

"I thought you said it did not matter if she rejected you, just so we could renew our relationship? So what do you do at her first rejection, but leave town without even telling us goodbye. Do you think that does anything to convince us that you are who you claim to be? I hope you're not going to try to see her on your way back to California! Can I conclude anything else except that your whole concern was to find her! And you weren't even patient enough to wait for me to try to help you!"

"I know it makes me look bad," he admitted, "but her words last night cut me to the heart! She said that she never wanted to see me, regardless of the circumstances, regardless of any change in my life. She said that as far as she was concerned, I am dead!"

"What did you expect her to say? Can you blame her? Do you expect everyone in this world to drop all they are doing and come running at the snap of your fingers, especially someone you treated in such a godless manner for so many years?"

He shrugged his shoulders and said nothing.

"You've even made me doubt your claim to be Ira Pointer!" I stated. "Who are you, really? If you're not Ira Pointer, why did you want to see my mother so badly?"

"I'm sorry, son. I guess I was just so crushed....." he offered as his head bowed and he began to cry once again.

I found myself going from certainty that he was not my father to wondering if he was. I couldn't let him go or I would never know for certain.

"Look! Can you stay here for a week or so? Maybe I can talk to her. But promise me you will not try to contact her again!"

He promised, and he cashed his bus ticket, and I took him back to the motel. I must confess that I wondered if I should have let him go ahead and leave. Could I be opening myself and my mother to further sorrow, even something that could hurt our relationship as mother and son?

When I got back to the office, I sat awhile wondering if this was the time to call my mother, and what I should say if I were to call her? Also, to be honest, I was trying to muster up the nerve to do so.

Then the Lord took care of the matter, as He often does. The phone rang, and it was mother calling me. She sounded pleasant, and then she said.

"Do you think this man is your father, Ira?"

I shared with her my mixed emotions over the whole situation.

"Sometimes I think he is, and other times I don't think so!" I admitted.

"Well, I'm coming to visit you, and we will put this matter to rest once and for all! As I thought about it last night, I realized I needed to do this for your sake. You need to know, even if I don't care if it is Ira Pointer. I shut and locked that door in my life years ago, and blocked it with a giant boulder. But I know that you need the truth. I'll be there by this evening. Meet me at the airport in Seminary City. I'll know whether he's Ira Pointer or not!! And either way, this man is in deep trouble!!"

I didn't like the sound of that last statement, but I did understand it, and hoped its bark was worse than its bite. At this point not much could have sent me into any deeper concern and shock, but would you believe me that it happened, though I could never have anticipated it.

Yes, the phone rang, and upon answering it, someone said, "I hear you're looking for me! My name is William Flagler, but I'm really Ira Pointer, and I will be arriving at Seminary City by plane. I must see you right away!"

What a shock! I had gone thirty years without knowing an Ira Pointer (except me), and now I had two guys in two days staking a claim to that name.

What in the world was going on?

What will my mother think of this?

And why did all these guys want to be Ira Pointer?

But that wasn't the worst of it! When I asked him on what plane he would arrive, I found out he would be on the same plane as my mother!!

Wow! Now that could be interesting! Or dangerous! Or both!!

Could This Get Any Worse?

I could hardly contain myself (and not in a good way), when I got off the phone. This was getting more confusing than eschatology! And probably more dangerous. And I had found out that eschatology can be dangerous. I shuddered to think of what might happen, if mother and this guy were to recognize one another, being on the same airplane!

I had to get my mind off of this strangely approaching scenario, so I brought out my books once again. I was beginning to wonder if I was using this study as an escape from the strife and anxiety of the search for my father. But maybe I needed that relief!

I could hardly keep myself in the books, but I determined that since I had presented the pre-mil conviction, and two preterist positions (the post-mil preterist view and the a-mil preterist view) that my next step would be to present the a-mil historical view. I found a book which summarized the position very clearly.[1]

The A-mil Historical View of Revelation

The author first gave what he considered to be some clear principles for interpreting the book of Revelation:

1. The main purpose of the book of Revelation is to comfort the persecuted believer.

2. The theme of the book of Revelation is the victory of Christ over Satan and his helpers.

3. The book of Revelation consists of seven sections, which are parallel, with each covering the same time span from the first to the second coming of Christ.

4. The seals, trumpets, bowls of wrath and other symbols refer not to specific events and details of history, but to principles of human conduct and moral government which are in operation throughout the history of the world, especially in the new dispensation.

5. The book of Revelation is to be interpreted in light of the conditions which were present when the book was written.

6. The book of Revelation is rooted in the sacred Scriptures, and therefore must be interpreted in harmony with the entire Bible.

7. The book of Revelation is the revelation of God, and therefore contains the purpose of God concerning the history of the church.

The author then gave a synopsis of the whole book of Revelation as follows.

I   CHAPTERS 1-3

We see Christ in the midst of His church
    the church is none other than a lampstand
    bearing the light of Christ to the dark world.
But whenever this happens
    the world hates the church
    and the result is Chapters 4-7

II CHAPTERS 4-7

The darkness of the world fights against the light
    the darkness hates the church
    the darkness refuses to be conquered by the light
    the darkness persecutes the light
The light suffers every kind of trial
    at the hand of the darkness
The whole events in this world, however,
    are over-ruled for the good of the church
    by the One on the Throne
The throne is ever in heaven---not on this earth
Believers are ever victorious
    as they come out of the great tribulation
        victorious in Christ

III CHAPTERS 8-11

The persecuted church prays to the Lord
    in the hour of her tribulation
The Lord hears and answers
    the prayers of His persecuted people
The Lord sees the blood of His martyred saints
    hence the trumpets of judgment
        warn the wicked

IV CHAPTERS 12-14

The struggle on the earth
between the church and the world
indicates a deeper struggle
between Christ and Satan

V CHAPTERS 15-16

The bowls of wrath always fall
upon the world for its treatment of the church

VI CHAPTERS 17-22

Satan and all his helpers seem to be victorious
but in reality they are always defeated

I wanted to go on and develop this a little more, but it was time to head for the airport. I surely would not want to be late for this arrival. I didn't know whether I would be picking up the pieces of a giant fight, or introducing two strangers. And then, I might have to pick up the pieces, as mother was introduced to another Ira Pointer!

I could have wondered how I could ever get myself into these messes, but the providence of God was my comfort and strength in this hour.

I did pick up Dink for moral support, and away we sped to the airport, while I tried to explain to him the latest circumstances in this revolving mello-drama. The king of the writer of soap operas couldn't duplicate this.

---

[1]Hendrikson, William, *More Than Conquerors* (Baker Book House, Copyright 1940 and 1967).

Will They Recognize One Another?

When we got to the gate at the airport, we were told the plane would be about thirty minutes late. That didn't help my state at all! So I paced up and down the airport aisle. Dink tried to settle me, but nothing would help! I didn't know how I would react to this second Ira Pointer, or William Flagler, or whoever he was.

Then I saw the plane pulling in towards the exit tube. I began wondering how I would recognize this guy. He said he would be wearing a plaid sports coat with a bow tie, so I decided that should not be too difficult to spot.

But then the horrible thoughts came back. Suppose they had sat by one another! Suppose they had recognized one another! Talk about a cat fight! Suppose they had not recognized one another! What will mother say, when I tell her who he claims to be? Suppose she concludes that there is no way possible he could be Ira Pointer, and begins to upbraid him in public---verbally and bodily!

I didn't know who I wished would get off first, but there she was, with no bow tie guy in sight. We greeted one another, and she seemed very happy, so I concluded nothing had happened on the plane! I continued looking for the bow-tie guy!

When I told her we needed to wait for someone else, understandably, she was curious as to whom it might be. She never could have guessed! I decided to wait and see if they recognized one another.

Then I spied him---the guy in the plaid coat and bow tie. I wondered if that had been Ira Pointer's favorite wardrobe from the past, and if that would ring a bell (good or bad) with mother.

I gulped when she saw him in the distance, and she remarked, sure enough, that a plaid coat and a bow tie had been my father's habit. I really got scared now, but I still said nothing, while waiting for the potential sparks to fly.

When he approached us, I flagged him down, and said, "Sir, I think you are looking for me!"

His dark brown eyes lit up, as he looked me over, but mother didn't say a word. It was clear that she did not recognize him as Ira Pointer. I asked if I could see him alone for a moment, and in that moment told him of the unique providence of God that had brought him and Ira Pointer's former wife to Seminary City on the same plane.

"Do you recognize her?" I asked.

He shook his head no, but then said, "Its been a long, long time."

"Well do you mind if I don't introduce you as Ira Pointer, because thus far she hasn't recognized you either, and I don't want a scene in the airport. After the way Ira Pointer treated her, there's no telling what she might do!"

He agreed, but then I gave him some more bad news.

"Do you realize that there is another man in my city right now who claims to be Ira Pointer?"

"You're kidding?" he spoke with his shock evident.

"Yes, don't you think its strange that for thirty years the only Ira Pointer I knew was me, and now in two days, I meet two more who claim that name?" I offered.

"You've got a point there. But I do look forward, Ira, to speaking to you privately about this matter, and convincing you who I am. I am really Ira Pointer---your father!"

"I've heard that one before!" I blurted out unconvinced, but with a smile.

We made our way through the baggage experience, and to the car, and I couldn't ask mother to sit in the back seat with him. So I asked Dink to drive, and I sat with her.

The conversation was fairly free, and he learned much about her (most I assumed he already knew), and she learned much about him. He claimed to be in oil in Texas, and by they way he talked, he had plenty of dough! They seemed to get along with one another quite well, with mother not suspecting anything. He was careful not to ask any questions which might upset the apple cart.

We took him to a different motel (no need for him to meet the other Ira Pointer at this point). Then after letting Dink out, we drove to my house, as mother would stay with us. I thought this was as good a time as any to tell her.

"Mother, I need to tell you something!" I began gingerly.

"Anything you wish, Ira!"

"Well, yesterday when I talked with you, we had one man claiming to be Ira Pointer. Now we have two men in town making the same claim."

"No!" she said with unbelief.

I didn't know what else to do, so I blurted it out!

"Yes, and the second one just got out of this car!"

I braced myself for the explosion, but it never came.

"You know, Ira! I thought in the airport that he might pass for the real Ira Pointer in his late fifties!"

"You what?" I asked .

"Well, he's the same height. Weight changes most in those years between the twenties and fifties, so that can't help us. He has brown eyes, like your father. He has an air of confidence, which was a definite characteristic of the real Ira Pointer. And the bow tie and plaid coat! If he's an imposter, he's a good one down to the very clothing he was wearing when we met, and also when I last saw him!

Then I remembered that the bow tie and plaid jacket routine was in the picture Samuel Seavers had given me. I thought at the time it was just old timey. Maybe it was more---a preference he would never change regardless of the style changes. Or maybe it was a ploy to fool us, hoping it would convince us as to his real identity.

"I thought you might be upset over this?" I probed.

"No, son, I came for your sake, not mine. I am dead to Ira Pointer! Too much water under the bridge. Too many nights crying to open anew any possibility of another heartbreak. I am perfectly satisfied with what the Lord has done and is doing in my life. And I assure you that I have no spirit of revenge against either of these men."

I gave a sigh of relief.

"But I will tell you one thing!" she continued. "Though I will not mistreat them, I do want to see their faces when they are exposed as imposters!"

"What if one is not exposed as an imposter, but is shown to be the real Ira Pointer?"

"That will be all right also. I'll tell him I have forgiven him, and that God, in spite of his sin, has given me the finest son any woman could ever want, and that I am living with Christ for the future, not for the past! I'll tell him goodbye, God bless you, but nothing more can ever be!"

She wasn't finished.

"In fact, I think I will enjoy this cat and mouse game--- especially when they meet each other!"

She might enjoy it, but I didn't see how I could!

23

The A-mil Historical View of Revelation?

I didn't sleep very well that evening, and when I was wide awake at 5:00 AM, I thought I had just as well get up and study, seeing I probably would not get much time the next day!

I had already given a brief outline of the a-mil historical view of Revelation, so I decided to outline the view chapter by chapter.

The A-mil Historical View of Revelation

CHAPTER 1
1. Here is the revelation of Jesus Christ   1-6
     which God gave to John
     which God signified to John by an angel
     which brings a blessing
         to the one who hears the prophecy
         to the one keeping the words
             of the prophecy
     which is sent to the seven churches
         in Asia Minor
         with the salutation of grace and peace
2. Here is the declaration of Christ's coming   7
     He comes with the clouds
     He is seen by every eye
         even by those who pierced Him
     He is mourned by all the tribes
         of the earth

3. <u>Here is Christ's self-designation</u> 8
4 <u>Here is John's commission to write the book</u> 9-11
5. <u>Here is John's vision of the Son of Man</u> 12-16
6. <u>Here is the effect of the vision of Christ</u> 17-20

CHAPTERS 2-3
    These chapters contain seven epistles
       to seven literal churches in Asia
       in the same pattern
           of Salutation or Address
           of Christ's Self-designation
           of Commendation
           of Condemnation
           of Warning and Threat
           of Exhortation
           of Promise
    These epistles describe conditions in John's time
       which have existed throughout church history
       which exist today
       which existed and exist through the entire age
           of the church
    The church is in the world of darkness
       the church should shine in the midst of the darkness

CHAPTERS 4-7
    <u>Chapters 4-5 teach us</u>
       that the affairs of this world
           rest in the hands of God
              not in the hands of man
       that when the world is filled
           with flames of hatred and slaughter
           with the drenching of blood
           our gaze must be on the One on the throne

that the Lord reigns from His throne
>   Let all the world tremble!
that God has an eternal plan
>   as pictured in the seven sealed scrolls
that Christ alone is worthy to open the seals
>   of the eternal plan of God
>   for He has conquered through His blood

Chapter 6 reveals to us the opening of the seals
>   *Seal one---the rider on the white horse is Christ*
>   who is conquering now in this age
>   as He exercises his spiritual universal kingship
>   *Seal two---the rider on the red horse is persecution*
>   towards believers upon the earth
>   even the slaughter of believers
>   for where Christ rides forth
>   >   to conquer and extend His spiritual kingdom
>   >   there will be the persecution of believers
>   *Seal three---the rider on the black horse is poverty*
>   even economic hardship among believers
>   which is part of the tribulation
>   that believers will often face
>   on their way to eternal glory
>   as members of Christ's kingdom
>   *Seal four---the rider on the pale horse brings death*
>   *or warfare, famine, pestilence, and wild beasts,*
>   *which are symbolic of all universal woes which*
>   *believers suffer along with the rest of humanity*
>   *throughout this age*
>   these woes are used as instruments
>   by the Lord Jesus Christ
>   for the sanctification of His church
>   for the extension of His kingdom

Seal five---the souls of those who had been slaughtered for the Word of God and their own testimony for Christ
>these martyrs cry out for vengeance
>>on those who killed them
>as they wonder how long it will be
>>until the Holy God avenges their deaths
>and they are given assurance
>>that their prayers will be answered

Seal six---this is the final judgment day of God
>there is
>>the description of the final catastrophe
>>>at the end of the age
>>the dread and terror of a frightened race
>>>as it faces the final judgement of God
>>>>including kings, princes, officers, rich men, strong men, slave and freemen
>>as the entire godless world
>>>faces the wrath
>>>>of the One on the throne
>>>>of the Lamb

Chapter 7

The vision of John has carried the reader
>to the end of the age

The next vision of John concerns two matters
>*verses 1-8---the Church Militant*
>>a picture of the church of all ages
>>>both Old Testament and New Testament
>>a picture of the spiritual Israel
>>>not one of fleshly or national Israel
>*verses 9-17---the Church Triumphant*
>>a picture of the Church at the end of the age

as it stands triumphantly before God
a great multitude
which no man can number
which has been gathered
from all nations
from all kindreds
from all peoples
from all tongues
which worships God
who have come out of great tribulation
who have washed their robes
who have made themselves white
in the blood of the Lamb
who are cared for by the Lamb
Thus this section too carries the readers
through the history of the church
to the end of the age

CHAPTERS 8-11
With the opening of the seventh seal
we now have the seven trumpet judgments
which also takes us back
to view once more the panorama
of the history of the church
This period of the trumpet judgments
is parallel with the seals
symbolizing not single nor separate events
but woes that can be seen
any day of the year
in any part of the world
These trumpet judgments are retributive
punishing the wicked
for their opposition and persecution of the saints

calling the wicked to repentance
and warning them of their final doom
Trumpet One---Hail and fire mixed with blood which
destroys the third part of the earth, the third part
of the trees and all the green grass
Thus our Lord from His reign in heaven
afflicts the persecutors of His church
with various disasters on <u>the land</u>
in every age
Trumpet Two---What looked like a huge mountain all
ablaze is cast into the sea
Thus our Lord from His reign in heaven
afflicts the persecutors of His church
with various disasters on <u>the sea</u>
in every age also
Trumpet Three---A great star fell from heaven, burning
as though it were a lamp, and it fell upon the third
part of the rivers and waters
Thus our Lord from His reign in heaven
afflicts the persecutors of His church
with various disasters in every age
<u>on the rivers and waters</u>
The result will be bitter sorrow
in the hearts of the wicked
Trumpet Four---A third part of the sun, moon and stars
are smitten so that a third part of them was
darkened so that they shone not for a third part of
the day and the night likewise
Thus our Lord from His reign in heaven
afflicts the persecutors of His church
with various disasters
from the sun, moon and stars

*Intermission---the soaring eagle who speaks God's
    judgment*
  The declaration of greater woe to come
  from the remaining trumpets to be sounded
*Trumpet Five---A star falls from heaven, to whom is
given the key to the bottomless pit, which is opened
by this fallen star, whereby he lets loose violent
creatures onto the earth*
  I beheld Satan fallen as lightning from heaven.
   Luke 10:18
  This is a picture of Satan in this age
   having been defeated by Christ at Calvary
    he has lost his position
    he has lost his splendor
    he has been given the key
     to the bottomless pit---hell
    he turns loose the demons onto the earth
     pictured as locusts
      of horrible description
      of horrible power
  This pictures the powers and influences of hell
   which operate in the hearts and lives
    of wicked and evil men
    during the time of the church on earth
  These demon forces
   do not harm the vegetation
    but the men who have not been sealed
     by God
    for a period of time
     pictured by the symbolic number
     of five months
  Thus clearly terror and destruction
   are Satan's work

The first woe is past
there are two more woes to come
Trumpet Six---Four angels who are bound in the river
Euphrates are loosed
This is a description of war---all wars
which are carried on
by the powers of darkness
As these armies go forth in astronomic numbers
they have one purpose---to destroy
they kill one third of mankind
These wars are a punishment and a warning
for unbelievers
The general meaning of these trumpets is clear
as throughout the ages in the history of the church
Christ will continually punish the persecutors
of His church by disasters
both physical and spiritual
in every sphere of their lives
Yet is spite of all of these warnings
mankind in general does not repent
for the hearts of men are foolish and stubborn
and they continue to transgress His law
The persecuting world becomes an impenitent world

As my mind was engrossed and my pen was flying, I was suddenly aware that others in the house were beginning to stir. I was shocked to discover it was 7:30.

I kept writing a little more, hating to leave my pursuit, much like a sleeping man hates to leave his bed. But then my writing slumber was broken by the phone, something quite common. The voice was Dink's, and he was excited.

"Preacha, I saw dose two guy ta gedder dis mornin'!"

24

Won't This Roller Coaster Ever Stop?

I had heard Dink correctly, but I couldn't help my response.

"You saw what?"

"I saw dose two guys, Barwell and Flagler, at Pony's Restaurant jus' thirty minutes ago!" he said again with excitement.

"What were they doing there?" I asked stupidly.

"Dey was eatin' and talkin' ninety miles an hour---talkin, dat is!"

"Did they see you?" I asked.

"Nah, when I saw dem, I jus' turned quickly an walked outta da place! Dey had no idea dey were discovered!"

"Did you see them leave the restaurant?" I continued to probe.

"Yeah, ya know Pony's is close to da motel where Barwell is stayin,' so ole Flagler got inna cab and I followed him back ta his motel cross-town."

When I got off the phone, I busied myself trying to help with breakfast, as Terry had gotten up during my conversation with Dink. Quietly, I explained the situation to her, but told her not to tell mother. I wanted her to meet them both today, and assess them objectively, without any further questions in her mind concerning their honesty.

After breakfast, I got ready to take Mother to meet Mr. William Flagler, the bow-tie guy. I tried to discern all the possibilities regarding these two who were claiming to be Ira Pointer.

One could be Ira Pointer.

Both could not be Ira Pointer.

If one was and the other one wasn't, how did they know each other?

If neither one was, how did they know each other?

If they had known each other previously, regardless of whether one was legitimate or not, why did they both come to town at the same time and make the same claim?

The whole thing made no sense!

The only thing that we seemed to know, was that they knew each other before arriving in town, because their motels were quite a distance apart. Thus, it would have been almost an impossibility for them to be found in the same restaurant in a strange city, let alone talking so freely, in the wee hours of the morning, if they had not known each other previously.

Were they getting ready to put a masterful sting on us, as they tried to convince us that one of them was Ira Pointer? I had sent the name of Samuel Barwell to Mack Turnover to seek to trace a true identity, but it was too early to have any response.

When we finally got to my office at the church, I didn't know what to expect. I wondered when I could confront him with his acquaintance with Mr. Barwell, but as he spoke, it became apparent that I would not have to do so. He opened the conversation with a shocker.

"I'm sorry, but I have a confession to make! I am not Ira Pointer! I am an imposter!"

My response was surprising to everyone, I am sure.

"Whoa, Nelly!! Slow this horse down! Someone is going to get hurt, if we don't!" I warned.

He then went on to explain that he had known the real Ira Pointer years ago in prison, that is, Mr. Barwell. They were cellmates, and he came to know his life and story and habits and expressions with perfection. He used to imitate him, and they used to talk way into the night about their past lives.

He went on.

"When I asked him one day if he was ever going to look up his former wife, and try to find his son, he said no with an absoluteness that seemed final. I asked him if I could try to find you both, when I got out of prison. He agreed, and then we passed our time preparing me for that hour. At that time he had no interest, and was even very bitter against you both!"

"Why did you want to find us?" I asked him.

"To see if I could convince you I was Ira Pointer. It had become a game over those months---a challenge, like a ball player awaits his day in the world series," he explained. "We both got out of prison after about a year or so, but I got in trouble again, and spent the last twenty-eight years in prison. We lost track of each other, but I passed my time thinking about the challenge of a new identity in a family where I would be accepted and loved."

Accepted and loved? I didn't buy that. I wanted to ask him if he had intended to mooch off of us or swindle money out of Mother, but I didn't ask.

"How did you find out he was in town?" I asked rather ignorantly without thinking it through.

"Oh, that was easy. When I got off the plane last night, and you told me there was a man in town claiming to be Ira Pointer, I knew it had to be the real Ira Pointer---now Samuel Barwell. So I began calling around town to find the motel where he was staying. When I found him, we decided to have breakfast together, and discuss the whole situation. I figured I had no chance trying to convince you I was Ira Pointer, when the real one was in town."

I had to admit I was still puzzled and unconvinced concerning either one of these men. Dink handed me a note he had written, and while Flagler talked to mother, I read it.

"Preacha, neither one of dem is Ira Pointer! Dey's runnin' a sting on us."

Knowing Dink's gangster background and his nose for stings, I had to agree with him. But what was the sting? The only thing I could figure out was that they were hoping this confession by Flagler would carry some weight to convince us that Barwell was Ira Pointer, when he was not. But that made little sense, unless they expected us to believe the testimony of an ex-con. Perhaps they thought our emotions would be so upset, that we would forget about that, and open our arms to Barwell without proper verification or with limited evidence for his claim.

Well, at least we had eliminated one Ira Pointer from the campaign to claim his identity, but we were now back where we had started. We still had one man continuing to make the claim.

Then mother spoke up with a real shocker!

"Sir, I don't believe a word you are saying! You are Ira Pointer! Why are you denying this? Is this some cruel game you are playing to hurt us again, as if you haven't hurt us enough?"

The man dropped his head, and didn't speak for several seconds. Now I really didn't know what to think.

Dink summarized it well, when he said, "Da last thirty minutes dis roller coaster climbed a giant mountain, but now's we'se flyin' back down dat mountain faster dan ever. Hang on ever' body. Da ride ain't over yet!! Wow!"

25

More of the A-mil View of Revelation?

William Flagler never answered mother. He merely got up and said, "I think its time for me to go back to the motel."

When I asked him if he was Ira Pointer, as mother claimed, he only answered, "Sometimes I wish I was, but you must realize Ira Pointer is gone, and will never return."

I was puzzled by that statement. Did he mean that he had been Ira Pointer, but now in some sense Ira Pointer was gone, in that the change of identity had rendered it impossible for him to be Ira Pointer again? Or did he mean Ira Pointer was someone else who was gone, and did not want to become Ira Pointer again? Or did he mean that Ira Pointer was dead, and could never return to us?

There was silence as I took him back to the motel, while Dink took mother home. He said nothing helpful as we drove, but he did indicate again that he had no desire to talk about the matter further. I asked him his plans now, but his answer was that he did not know. I urged him to please call me tonight, but, seriously, I wondered if I would ever see him again. How do you make a man talk, when he does not want to talk?

I called mother when I arrived back at church, and she was still adamant that he was the real Ira Pointer! If that were so, I thought, the big fish was about to spit out the bait and swim away. When I called the motel, I found out I was right. He had already checked out and was gone! I was sure he was getting out of town. But why? Because he was

Ira Pointer, as mother said, or because he wasn't Ira Pointer, as he finally claimed?

I asked the motel clerk to refrain from cleaning the room, because I needed to get some fingerprints. He said that he would have to have a police order to do that.

I debated whether I should try to stop him at the airport, but I concluded that would be a waste of time, in light of his mood when I last saw him.

I wanted to talk to mother more deeply about the matter, but I decided I would give her a chance to settle down and analyze the situation before getting her thoughts.

I also called Samuel Barwell, halfway expecting him to have left town as well, but he was still there. I changed our meeting with him until evening. He didn't seem fazed when he learned Flagler had gone.

I was so frustrated over the matter, that I decided to spend the rest of the afternoon finishing the a-mil historical summary of the book of Revelation. That truly would be relaxing, in light of what I had been through!

SUMMARY OF THE A-MIL HISTORICAL VIEW OF REVELATION 1-11

The a-mil view we were summarizing said that the book of Revelation contains several movements of the history of the church. Each of these movements leads up to the end time.

Movement One---Chapters 2-3
   The Church exists throughout its history in a world of darkness and has the duty to shine the light of the gospel into that dark world in which it exists.

Movement Two---Chapters 4-7
> The Church throughout its history, though it passes
> through severe suffering and persecution in its
> militant state, will emerge triumphant because
> it is truly serving a risen and conquering Savior.

Movement Three---Chapters 8-11
> The church throughout its history can see how God
> punishes the evil doers, even though they do not
> repent, and remain hardened in heart against Him.

Again, the key to understanding this a-mil view is that it
claims to give a message to all the churches of all the
centuries of the history of the church; and not just a
message to the people of the first century, as claims the
preterist view; nor only to the people of the last few years
of the history of the church, as does the pre-mil view.

I now turned to summarize the remainder of the view of the
book of Revelation according to this a-mil conviction. In
these chapters we see again another view of the church as it
moves through its entire history. It carries us back to the
birth of Christ and carries us through to His final judgment
upon men of the earth.

CHAPTERS 12-14
> Chapter 12
>> The woman pictures the church
>>> in its OT/ NT stage
>>> for the church is one chosen people
>>>> of God
>> The mighty child, the seed of the woman, is Christ
>>> who is to rule the nations with a rod of iron

The dragon standing to devour the child at His birth
is Satan who through all of human history
has sought to destroy the seed of the woman
both before His birth and after His birth
The child was caught up to God and to His throne
following His victory over Satan at the cross
The woman now flees into the wilderness
as Satan continues his attack on the church
when he failed to defeat Christ
but God protects the church in the wilderness
Chapter 13
The agents Satan uses to attack the church
are shown in this chapter
THE BEAST OUT OF THE SEA
pictures the persecuting power of Satan
embodied in all the governments
of the world throughout history
THE BEAST OUT OF THE EARTH
symbolizes false religion and philosophy
which cause men to exalt and follow
an antichristian government
which seeks to place itself
on the throne of God

Chapter 14
The triumph of God's church at end of the age
The Lamb on Mt. Zion
standing with the sealed multitude
of chapter 7
enjoying the blessedness of heaven
after the final judgment
having persevered victoriously
in the face of the dragon
singing a new song

<u>The angel announcing the hour of judgment</u>
    to those at ease on the earth
<u>The angel announcing the fall of Babylon</u>
    the destruction of apostasy
<u>The angel announcing judgment with clarity</u>
    upon those who have served Satan
<u>The voice from heaven announcing</u>
    the blessedness of the dead
      who die from henceforth
        as they see the Lord face to face
<u>The arrival of the judgment of the wicked</u>
    the winepress of God's wrath
      is trodden down
        resulting in bloody death
        upon the wicked

Thus again the a-mil would say that we have seen a picture of the history of the church through history, centering upon Christ and His church as opposed by the great enemy, Satan, to the final judgment of the wicked.

At this point I decided I had better get going to pick up mother and meet Mr. Barwell. I wondered if he would still be there, or if he too had skipped town. I wondered also if he knew of our conversation with Flagler, and if he would still be proclaiming his identity as that of Ira Pointer.

Then it hit me---perhaps the key I had been seeking. I thought of a question that I could ask him that would immediately tell me if he wasn't Ira Pointer. It might not tell me he was Ira Pointer, but his answer would assure me he was not the man he claimed to be, if he answered it incorrectly!

Maybe we were getting somewhere after all!

26

Are We Stymied Again?

When I stopped by my house to pick up my mother, I found her still convinced that William Flagler was the real Ira Pointer. She was willing to go with me to quiz Samuel Barwell, but nothing would change her mind concerning Flagler.

"What is it that convinced you beyond doubt that he is the real Ira Pointer, and after thirty years?" I asked, having no clue whatsoever to her thinking.

"Well, he looked like him, though older. He acted like him in mannerisms and expressions. He talked like him. He dressed like him!" she stated adamantly.

"But couldn't you have been fooled by a good con man in these areas?" I asked testing her.

"Yes, but none of those were the clincher for me!" she offered.

"What was, then? I can't think of anything else which might have persuaded you!" I prodded.

"Did you see the ring?" she asked.

"No, not really!" I replied.

"Did you see the wrist watch?" she continued.

"Yes, I saw that! Pretty fancy!" I admitted.

"Did you see the cuff links?" she snapped.

"Yes, and those were fancy also!" I noted.

"And did you see the tie clasp?" she added.

"Yes, it seems some of those items were a matched set, and kind of old, but still sharp!" I recalled.

"I gave all of those items to him some thirty years ago!!! Case settled!" she concluded.

"I don't know!" I mused. "Are these items conclusive?"

"Look, son! What man would keep those items all these years except a man like Ira Pointer. I know him. And just like the bow tie and the plaid jacket were his staples in dress, so were these other items."

"After thirty years?" I thought out loud.

"After thirty years!" she nodded firmly.

"Well, lets see what we can find out about this man Barwell now," I said, as we pulled up in front of the motel.

Barwell was ready and waiting, so we went for supper at a fairly fancy restaurant. After we were seated and had ordered, the discussion began.

"Mr. Barwell," I began, "are you aware of our conversation with Mr. Flagler this afternoon?" I asked.

"I suppose he told you that he was an imposter, and that I was the real Ira Pointer," he said nonchalantly.

"And what else did he tell us?" I continued.

"Well, I'm not sure, but probably that we had been in prison together, and that's where he got all the information about me and my family, as well as all the practice in acting and talking like me," he noted. "Surely, this will convince you that I am Ira Pointer!"

"Well, not quite!" I stated. "I have a key question yet for you to answer!"

"You have a key question?" he asked with a puzzled look.

He had been in total control with a cool attitude to this point. We were now moving outside of his realm of knowledge to an uncertain area and question.

He gathered himself and challenged, "Well, let's have it. What is that key question?"

"Mr. Barwell, did you ever write a book?" I stated, trying to keep from appearing that I was ambushing him.

"Yes, I did," he stated with certainty.

"What was the subject of the book?" I pressed on.

He appeared to have some concern now, as if he thought, I might know something he did not know.

"I believe it was some kind of religious book," he said with some hesitation now.

I thought to myself, could a man ever write a book sometime in his lifetime, and not even know the subject?

"What kind of a religious book?" I pursued relentlessly.

"Maybe on theology," he said, getting weaker and weaker as we proceeded. I had caught him completely by surprise.

"What area of theology?" I sought further.

"Maybe on God?" he said with perhaps some concern that his cover was being blown away now.

"Does the word 'eschatology' mean anything to you?" I asked. He was silent.

"Can you tell me what view a preterist holds in the area of eschatology?" I challenged again. No answer.

"Can you tell me what an a-mil is?" I hit him again.

"That was a long time ago!" he said seeking to excuse his ignorance.

"Okay, then, define one term that has to do with Bible prophecy?" I offered generously. Silence.

"What was the title of your book?" I tried him again.

It was obvious that he had never heard of the book, or if he had, he figured we did not know about it.

Silence prevailed as he hung his head, like a kid caught with his hand in the cookie jar.

Finally he made an admission.

"All right! I am not Ira Pointer. You talked with the real Ira Pointer this morning, and now he is gone! He was honest with you when he said we had been in prison together, but it was just the opposite of the picture he painted. He was the real Ira Pointer, and I was the one who dreamed of imitating him. I guess I either didn't do a very good job, or I underestimated the people I would need to convince," he said somewhat sorrowfully.

"But why?" I asked.

"Because I knew through the years as I was in jail, and he was out, that your mother, you Mrs. Pointer, were becoming a very rich lady in the nursing home business--- even a millionaire! I guess I thought I could convince you that I was Ira Pointer, and stir up a romance, so that I could get some of that money!" he admitted. "I didn't realize Pointer had written a book, and if he had, that you would know its content, or if you did that you would think to ask me about it. That's the one area we left uncovered."

I must admit that the statement that mother was a millionaire shocked me! I had no idea she was that wealthy, though she did have a beautiful home, a nice car, and dressed immaculately. But I had another question.

"We?" I asked. "Who is the 'we?'" I asked. "Does the we mean that the real Ira Pointer, alias William Flagler, was part of this con scheme?"

"No, the word 'we' is to speak of myself and another old prison friend. We planned all of this without Pointer's knowledge. I was to convince you that I was the real Ira Pointer for the money I could get. When the real Ira Pointer found out we were going to do this, he came to town to stop us. He was willing to come and reclaim his real identity and expose us! He had never desired to approach you previously, because he was uncertain of his acceptance, as he had hurt you both so much already."

"What stopped him from exposing you? Why did he at first claim to be Ira Pointer when he arrived, but denied that identity the next morning?" I asked.

"Well, he called me when he got to town, and told me he would not go along with our plan. I told him we would discuss it at breakfast, which we did. It was there that he decided to leave town, denying his claim!" he explained.

"Do you mean he was willing to let us be fooled and even robbed?" I asked. "What kind of a man is that?"

"Don't be too hard on your father! When the life of your wife and son, and even your own life are the marbles in the con game, would you have done differently?"

"Do you mean you threatened his life and ours?" I asked in shock.

He turned serious and stone cold!

"Yep, in a heartbeat! We will do anything for money!"

"Then why did you give up so easily in your little game?" I queried.

"You win some and you lose some. No use going on when you have lost, and you got me this time. I'll be leaving town immediately."

"What if we call the police?" I asked.

He laughed a devilish laugh, and countered, "I wouldn't do that, if I were you! We have friends who will be around to see you, if you do. I promise you, I'll leave town and you'll never see me again."

I wondered how good the promise of such a man was--- probably not much. I had to ask him one more question.

"Do you know where I can get in touch with Mr. Flagler, or Ira Pointer?"

"I have no idea! He's the slickest dude alive! I never can find him. He contacts me. He's on the go constantly."

"Where does he get the money?" I asked.

"Does a slick dude who is a con man and a master of disguise have to work for money? He could con a bear out of his hide. They tell me though that he has changed. He used to work with us some. We've made some big bucks together. But they say he got religion and is preaching too. Can you imagine---Ira Pointer a preacher again?"

I had some mixed emotions as I left Barwell at the motel. Was this the truth? Had I actually met my father, and talked with him? Should I have been more friendly towards him? And now was he gone forever?

Mother was struggling too. She was convinced he was the real Ira Pointer, and some of her hard-nosed attitude was beginning to fade. She too wished she could have had a straightforward discussion with the supposedly real Ira Pointer.

I kept asking myself if it could have been possible for my father to have been a con man all these years? I had hoped for better, but I guess I should not be surprised at anything in light of the way he had treated us. But even further, could it be possible that now he had been truly saved, and was serious about the ministry? Or was this just another con game for money?

I didn't have much confidence that I could ever trust him again. But maybe that was a moot question. We would have to find him first, and that seemed an impossibility! We were stymied again, it seemed.

I felt sad to think that perhaps he was my father, and I would never see him again!

27

Can We Finish the A-mil Historical View of Revelation?

When we arrived home, neither mother nor I had much desire to talk further about the day or evening's experience. I could sense that she needed some time alone to absorb it all, or maybe even to grieve to herself.

I spent the next hour or so sharing all the strange events surrounding the two Ira Pointers with Terry. I was even more amazed as I sought to explain it all to her! Finally we both fell off to sleep, though sleep that night was not easy.

Waking early, I decided to do some more work on the eschatology book. I had learned a long time ago to carry needed books with me, because one never knows when he might be confronted with a time frame for reading or labor.

I had not intended to spend so much time on the a-mil view, but interruptions had seemed to necessitate intervals for study and writing. I hoped no one who might read the book would think I was favoring this view.

I summarized the a-mil view of Revelation up to this point of my study.

The A-mil Historical View of Revelation 1-14

The a-mil view we were summarizing said that the book of Revelation contains several pictures (movements) of the history of the church. Each of these pictures leads up to the end time.

Movement One---Chapters 2-3
>The Church exists throughout its history in a world of darkness and has the duty to shine the light of the gospel into that dark world in which it exists.

Movement Two---Chapters 4-7
>The Church throughout its history, though it passes through severe suffering and persecution in its militant state, will emerge triumphant because it is truly serving a risen and conquering Savior.

Movement Three---Chapters 8-11
>The church throughout its history can see how God punishes the evil doers, even though they do not repent, and remain hardened in heart against Him.

Movement Four---Chapters 12-14
>The church throughout its history centering on Christ will be opposed by the great enemy, Satan and his helpers, but there is a final judgement coming for the wicked.

Again, the key to understanding this a-mil view is this. It claims to give a message to all the church of all the centuries of the history of the church. Thus it disagrees with the preterist view which makes the book, for the most part, a message to the people of the first century. It disagrees with the futurist view which makes the book, for the most part, a message to the people of the last few years of the history of the church. These statements should not be taken as any argument for the a-mil view, but just some observations.

Revelation 15-22

CHAPTERS 15-16

This section shows clearly that when the wicked fail to repent when facing God's partial manifestation of judgment, the final and further wrath of God will still follow.

The vision of the bowls of judgment, though also covering the entire age of the church, is especially applicable to the final day of judgment and the days which will immediately precede it.

These are the seven last plagues which will smite those who have the mark of the beast and worship his image.

The seven bowls of God's final judgment include:

1. Bowl One---foul and painful sores
2. Bowl Two---the sea becoming like the blood of a dead man
   and every living soul in the sea dying
3. Bowl Three---the rivers and fountains of water become blood
4. Bowl Four---the sun scorching men
   man's response---still no repentance
5. Bowl Five---the beast's kingdom is full of darkness
   so that men gnaw their tongues for pain
   so that men blaspheme God
6. Bowl Six---the way is cleared for sinful men to come and make war against God
   (Prior to the seventh bowl of judgment three un-clean spirits come forth out of the mouths of the dragon [Satan], the beast [anti-Christian government], and the false prophet [anti-Christian religion]).
7. Bowl Seven---the final judgment day arrives

CHAPTERS 17-19
<u>Chapter 17</u>
This chapter describes the history
of Babylon---
the great harlot
From the description given in this chapter
Babylon pictures the world
as the center of seduction
at any moment of history
but particularly at the end of the age
<u>Chapter 18</u>
This chapter shows the complete and final fall
of Babylon
The fall of Babylon takes place throughout history
but especially and finally at the final judgment
The work of Babylon is to seduce and persecute
the saints of God of history
the saints of God in the final days
<u>Chapter 19</u>
This chapter shows the following:
the rejoicing in heaven due to Babylon's fall
the marriage supper of the Lamb and His bride
the Author of the fall as He comes in judgment
against Babylon
against the beast
against the false prophet
against all His enemies
Thus these chapters traverse the same ground
of the previous movements seen
in the book of Revelation
that is the entirety of the church's history

CHAPTERS 20-22
    These chapters also traverse the same ground
        of the previous movements
           which we have seen
               in the book of Revelation
                   that is the entire history of the church
                   yet from a different aspect

<u>Chapter 20</u>
    This chapter speaks
        of the binding of Satan
           at the first coming of Christ
        of the final defeat of Satan
           and all of his enemies
           at the second coming of Christ

1. <u>he was bound at Christ's first coming</u> 1-3
        it is for the era of the church age
           as pictured in the one thousand years
        it is to protect the church
           to allow the great missionary work
        it is not a complete binding of Satan
           he still possess influence
           but he can deceive the nations no more
               as in the Old Testament period
               as the world is opened to the gospel
           he has a paralyzed influence
           in that sense

2. <u>he is bound but the saints reign with Christ</u> 4-6
        the reign with Christ
           is in heaven
           not on the earth
           thus this too speaks of the present age

the reign is that of those who died for Christ
the saints martyred for Christ
during the history of the church
the saints who died in their faith
all other believers
the reign is not in bodily form but as souls
until Christ's second coming
this is the first resurrection
that is the translation of the soul at death
from earth to God's holy heaven
the second resurrection includes the bodies
of both the saved and the lost
as the saints' bodies are reunited
with their souls (see above)
as the lost's bodies are reunited also
with their souls

3. <u>he is loosed after the thousand years</u> 7-10
for his final attack upon believers
this is the same battles as described
in Revelation 16:12ff
in Revelation 19:19ff
for the final defeat of his forces
at Christ's second coming
same as pictured in Revelation 19
for his final defeat
as he is cast into the lake of fire

4. <u>his followers are cast into hell</u> 11-15
Christ is on the throne
at the final day of divine judgment
the dead small and great
stand before Him

            all are judged
                by the Lamb's book of life
                by the record books of every man's life
            this is one general resurrection
                for all men of all ages
            death and hell are cast into the lack of fire
                all whose names are not written
                    in the Lamb's book of life
                    are also cast into the lack of fire

CHAPTERS 21-22

Chapter 21:1-22:5

    The new heaven and the new earth is seen
        a reference to fully redeemed humanity
        after the judgment day has come
    The New Jerusalem comes down from heaven
        this is the church of the Lord Jesus Christ
        (a bride adorned for her husband)
        where there will be eternal fellowship with God
            completed sorrow---no tears
            constant worship---no break of fellowship
            continuing life---no death
    all things are made new
        by the One sitting on the throne

Chapter 22:6-22

    Final attestations, admonitions and promises

I was interrupted by mother as she came into the living room where I was working.

"Ira, I have made a decision during the night!" she declared.

"Oh?" I said simply, not knowing she was going to make a speech, and one which surprised me, I must admit.

"I am giving up this search for Ira Pointer. I never was too much involved in it, except for your part. But I must admit that I may have gotten emotionally involved the past few days. God renewed my peace last night. Something of the hope and memory of one's youth returns at an interval of life like this. But I have decided that it is no more than that---a youthful hope, which in one's youth may have had some value and some possibility of reality, but which once lost, yea even destroyed, becomes a foolish and impossible hopelessness, which can never rise again in the same manner as in the past."

I was shocked at her depth of understanding of the factors in our search, and her ability to communicate them.

She continued.

"We humans seem to desire to live in the past, not realizing that the passing of years can often transform a hopeful past into a hopeless future. I think we found a man who years ago was Ira Pointer, a man who knew who he was and where he was going. But today we found a man who transverses the earth like the wind, not knowing whither he comes nor whither he goes---an empty shell of a man in comparison to his early days. Yes, I feel sorrow for him, but not for myself, for my years have been far more rewarding to me than his to him, and even so now."

I certainly agreed with her, and even wondered if my participation in such a search for my father would have been better left alone also.

I concluded that the search was over---we had found him. But as mother had indicated, what had we found? Really? More grief.

Mother said she wanted to go home the next morning. So we changed her ticket and put her on the plane. There was a sadness as we parted, but a thankfulness we had found each other. We both were excited about building on that rediscovered foundation.

I still felt somewhat empty as I drove home by myself. I couldn't help wondering where Ira Pointer was, and what he was doing? Was it another scam? Or was he preaching somewhere? And most of all, was he really my father? Only God knew! It seemed the door now was closed as tight as before, never to be reopened! Or so I thought!

I turned again to a chart of the <u>a-mil view</u>.

The A-mil View of the Movements of Church History
(Not all a-mils would see the movements in exact manner)

NT Church History
(Note that each section covers all of church history)

MOVEMENT ONE
--------Chpts 2-3---The Church as the light of a dark world--------

MOVEMENT TWO
--------Chpts 4-7---The Church triumphant in persecution---------

MOVEMENT THREE
----Chpts 8-11---The Church in an unrepentant world which is---
under God's judgment

MOVEMENT FOUR
------Chpts 12-14---The Church opposed by Satan but final-------
judgment will come

MOVEMENT FIVE
------------Chpts 15-19---The Church sees the judgment-----------
on a Christ-rejecting world

MOVEMENT SIX
----------Chpts 20-22---The Church in its final victory!------------

28

Can You Summarize All These Views ?

During the next few days, I tried to summarize the various views of the book of Revelation that I had pursued. I made the following notes concerning each view.

The Pre-mil View

This was a <u>futurist understanding</u> of the book. That is, for the most part, the book of Revelation is yet to be fulfilled. The first chapter contains what John had seen, chapters 2-3 presented the present, and chapters 4-22 present the future even from our stand point. Those chapters (4-22) center on the tribulation period of seven years, when the Antichrist would rise to power and persecute the people of God. He would rule ruthlessly for a period of three and a half years, having taken the first three and a half years to attain full control of the earth. God's judgment is also poured forth on the earth during this time. Christ will come according to chapter 19, and then He will reign upon this earth for a thousand years, according to chapter 20. Also in chapter 20, the lost will be judged, and then in chapters 21-22 the saved will have the privilege of eternity with Christ.

I also noted that pre-mils were divided as to whether the church would go through this tribulation period. <u>Dispensational pre-mils</u> think the church will be raptured in chapter 4 at the beginning of the tribulation period (pre-trib rapturists), while <u>historic pre-mils</u> and <u>covenantal pre-mils</u>

believe in a post-trib rapture in chapter 19, just before the Second Coming of Christ (post-trib rapturists), while still others hold to a rapture in the middle of the tribulation period in chapter 11 (mid-trib rapturists).

The Post-mil View

The post-mil view which we have considered involves those who hold a preterist conviction of the book of Revelation (most of Revelation was fulfilled by the time of the fall of Jerusalem in 70 AD). Yet all post-mils hold some things in common.

The kingdom is a literal earthly kingdom which will be brought in by the preaching of the gospel during this age. Though not all will be converted, the peoples of the earth will be Christianized as a great multitude of the population of the earth will be saved. The power of Christ will bring the kingdom through the gospel, and then at the end of the kingdom period Christ will return to the earth visibly, when there will then be one resurrection of the dead, one final general judgment of all men, to be followed by a new heaven and new earth.. The time of the kingdom will not be a literal one thousand year period, but a lengthy period of time.

Also, more particularly, the preterists, would believe in the general scheme just outlined above. But as preterists, they would believe further that most of the book of Revelation was fulfilled during the days leading up to and during the fall of the city of Jerusalem in 70 AD. Still others, including many of the preterists, would also embrace a view known as theonomy, which puts great emphasis on the application of the law of God upon all of society, as the gospel conquers the earth, bringing a society with Christian morals, values and laws.

The A-mil View

The a-mil view believes the kingdom of Christ is a spiritual kingdom which was inaugurated at His death, and will continue until His second coming. Thus there will be no literal earthly millennium or kingdom. Christ is ruling over the earth now from His throne in heaven. Furthermore, Satan is now bound because of the victory of Christ, but that does not mean he has lost his influence, nor that there is no spiritual battle. It means he is no longer able to keep the gospel from going out to all the world.

The a-mil believes also that the present age will end with a form of tribulation and apostasy, and with the appearance of an antichrist, and the universal preaching of the gospel with many being saved, including a great number of Jews. The great spiritual battle between Christ and Satan will end with His second coming, which will be followed by a general resurrection and judgment.

The a-mil view believes the following: that the New Testament church is the new Israel; and that the saints of all ages are in the body of Christ; and that the New Testament form of the church is the new Israel with many of the promises of God to His people in the Old Testament being fulfilled in the New Covenant church.

The a-mil view has some divisions within it, as follows: some a-mils are preterists (the book of Revelation was fulfilled for the most part during and at the fall of Jerusalem in 70 AD), and some are historicists (the book of Revelation pictures the continual unfolding of the church in history in several movements in the book of Revelation).

I determined at this point that I would see how each of these views handled Matthew 24, another important part of the prophetic witness of the Bible.

As I was resting for a few moments, the usual interruption came. It was Mack Turnover. He had given the names of Samuel Barwell and William Flagler to his investigators, and wanted to tell me what they had found.

"You won't believe it, Ira!" he began with some excitement in his voice.

That's all I needed on this subject right now, was someone who knew something that I did not know. I kindly encouraged him to get on with it!

"I'm sorry, Pastor Ira. I should realize you are exhausted from all of this, and I should give you my information immediately!"

I wanted to say, "Then why don't you?" But grace prevailed, and I waited patiently and silently.

"Well, Samuel Barwell was killed this morning, and they have arrested William Flagler (or Ira Pointer, perhaps) on the murder charge! He asked us to contact you and tell you that he wants to see you!"

"Where is he!" I queried.

"He's in Texas. It seems that they both went there after leaving your city those several days ago."

"Does Mr. Flagler have an alibi?" I asked.

"Not at all!" he answered. "In fact, they found the murder weapon, and it's a gun which belongs to him! Yet he vows he did not do it! He asked me to call you and tell you that he needs your help."

I thought to myself, "I'll bet he does! But did I dare get involved, not knowing his real identity?"

29

The Pre-mil View of Matthew 24?

After discussing the matter with Terry, and after sharing the news with my mother, I decided to go to Texas to see William Flagler. Dink volunteered to go, as Mack Turnover had offered to pay for two plane tickets. Obviously, mother did not want to go, but Dink was ready and eager. Later that day we were on our way to the airport at Seminary City.

As we drove, I admitted to Dink that there were some questions bothering me.

"Yeah, Preacha, I can imagine. I got some questions, too. Tell me yours and then I'll tell ya mine," he offered.

"Well, for the first thing, what were they doing in the same city? They left here rather disgruntled towards one another. Why did they go to the same city?" I asked.

"Preacha, dey couldda been in da same city fer several reasons. Maybe dey was scammin' ya! Maybe Flagler, whether he was yer dad or not, decided he wanted to back out on da scam, since he'd gotten ta know you and yer mother. Maybe he felt some love and kinship to you, an didn't wantta carry it through. Maybe dat led to a fight, and Flagler killed Barwell."

"Yes, that's possible!" I agreed.

"On da other hand, maybe Flagler, whether he was yer dad or not again, wasn't in on the scam to begin with, and decided to get a cut of the money Barwell hoped to get."

"Dink, there are a lot of possibilities, aren't there. How will we ever know the truth, unless God somehow reveals it to us?"

"Yeh, dat's fer sure!" he agreed.

"But when, and how?" I wondered to myself.

As we flew, I decided to begin looking at Matthew 24 by considering the pre-mil view. Notice that each position is noted as "A…" not "The…" This indicates that there are differing interpretations even among scholars in each category of views.

A Historic Pre-mil View of Matthew 24[1]

I had arrived at two conclusions in my study of this chapter of Matthew. First, that it is a very difficult passage, and secondly, there is no single pre-mil interpretation of Matthew 24. I decided to give one of the clearest to my understanding. Notice should be taken of the following in seeking to unravel this chapter, according to the historic pre-mil view.

First, the disciples' questions indicate clearly that they think of the destruction of Jerusalem and the Second Coming of Christ as one single event. Thus they ask:

Question One
"Tell us when shall these things be?" (a reference to the destruction of Jerusalem in light of Christ's statement in verse 2 that there will not be left one stone upon another)

Question Two

"And what shall be the sign of thy coming, and of the end of the age?" (a reference to the Second Coming of Christ)

<u>Second</u>, the disciples are given an answer by Christ which speaks of both events, that is, the fall of Jerusalem and the Second Coming at the end of the age.

The Whole Period Characterized 24:4-28

The whole period between the time Christ speaks and His Second Coming will be a difficult time of persecution and affliction and tribulation for His disciples.

A Part of the Period is Pictured 24:15-21

Within the larger period, which pictures the time between the time Christ's speaks in Matthew and His Second Coming, is a very severe and horrible time of persecution and tribulation, that is, the fall of Jerusalem at 70 AD, as pictured in 24:15-21.

The Second Coming Is to Follow 24:29-31

Obviously there is some delay between the heavy and violent time of the persecution at the time of the fall of Jerusalem and the Second Coming. Remember that verses 15-21 fit into the whole period found in verses 4-28. Then verses 29-31 speak of the Second Coming of Christ. Thus Christ answers the disciples' questions, and the answer Christ gives is applicable to the disciples and the people of their day (the reference to the fall of Jerusalem), and to future generations beyond the fall of

Jerusalem (the reference to the Second Coming of Christ).

A Dispensational Pre-mil View of Matthew 24[2]

The disciples actually have three questions in the early verses of this chapter:

1. Questions One---When will these things be? 24:3

   This is a reference to the destruction of Jerusalem which was fulfilled in 70 AD. This question is answered in Luke 21:20-24. Matthew 24 does not answer this question.

2. Questions Two and Three---What will be the sign of Your coming and the end of this age? 24:3

   These questions are answered in Matthew 24:4-33. A description of Israel's time of trouble at the end of the age is in verses Matthew 24:9-28, and the account of the Messiah coming to appear to Israel is found in 24:29-25:30. Thus these verses speak of the end time, and not the fall of Jerusalem. The rapture is not mentioned in this section of Scripture, nor is there any reference to the church or to the Holy Spirit.

As I came to the end of these notes, I rested my head back on the seat as we flew through the skies. I couldn't help making a comparison between my search for my father and my theological pursuit of eschatology.

Both were very difficult. Both required careful study of the data. Both could involve misinterpretation of the data, and thus allow errors of understanding. Both could allow a false certainty of a conviction, if one looked only at part of the data. Both could allow deception in a conclusion, if only part of the data was considered. Both required a full knowledge of the data and its implications, before a conclusion could be drawn. Both could leave one cold towards the pursuit, thinking maybe that the search was hopeless.

I had strong convictions towards eschatology when that search began, and they were remaining firm. But I had to admit that I was grateful to gain knowledge of the other positions, which gave me a greater appreciation of them, and less of a spirit of antagonism towards them.

But in this regard my pursuit of my father was different. I had been like a yo-yo on a string, as men had jerked me around all over the place. To be honest, even at this moment, as I flew to talk to William Flagler, the man who seemed to have the greatest evidence backing his claim, I was totally baffled as to the identity of my father. I wondered if we had even come close to finding him.

Then I remembered my question which had tripped up Barwell---the one about my father's book. I decided I would ask the same question to Flagler to get his reaction.

Maybe I was getting closer to his identity! But if he was my father, who wanted a murderer for a father?

---

[1]D. A. Carson, "Matthew," *Expositor's Bible Commentary*, Volume 8 (Grand Rapids: Regency Reference Library, Zondervan Publishing House, 1984), p. 495.

[2]"The Olivet Discourse," *New Unger's Bible Dictionary* (Chicago, Ill: Moody Press, 1988).

30

Has the Search Been Worth It?

When we finally arrived that evening at the jail, a small town county jail, they didn't want to let me see Mr. Flagler. I finally convinced them by explaining, that I thought he might be my father. They probably thought it strange, that here was a guy who didn't even know his father, yet was trying to claim a guy for that honor, who was charged with murder.

When we were able to see him, his manner was very humble and broken. He was very appreciative of our coming, thanking us a half-dozen times or more.

Then I asked him, "What happened? Are you really being held for murder?"

"Yes, but I didn't kill anyone, let alone Barwell!" he pled. "And besides that, they have no body---only a witness who said I did it!"

"No body, but you're being held for murder?" I asked quite puzzled.

"Yes, it beats anything I ever saw!" he answered with some bewilderment.

He then told us that he came to this town to confront Barwell about the scam. He wanted to plead with him to stop it. He claimed his heart had been broken by meeting his son and former wife, and felt that he might make up for some of his past neglect towards us by scuttling Barwell's plans. At this point he began to cry.

He continued the story further.

"Barlow and I met on a pier in the gulf, and argued violently and loudly for a good while. Then, a witness says I drew a gun and shot him, and he fell into the gulf!"

"You shot him, and he fell into the gulf?" I asked. "Is that the way it happened?"

"NO!" he protested! "He shot at me, and was trying to kill me, but he slipped and fell backwards into the gulf! He shot at me! I did not shoot at him!"

"And they haven't found the body?" I asked.

"No!" he replied.

"Then why did they arrest you?" I asked.

"Because they found my gun at the bottom of the gulf not far from where Barwell fell!" he explained.

Dink stepped in to try to get some clarity.

"Ya didn't shoot him?"

"No!"

"Ya didn't shoot at him?"

"No!"

"Ya didn't try to kill him?"

"No!"

"He shot at you!"

"Yes!"

"He tried to kill you? Dey found da gun---yer gun---but not da body?"

"Yes!"

"Dey arrested you widdout a body and only da gun an' da word a one witness?"

"Yes."

"Is dat all?"

"No, my gun had been fired and there were two bullets missing, the number of shots the witness heard!"

"Was da witness close!"

"Well, fairly!"

"What's fairly?"

"Fifty feet!"

"Was it dark?"

"About dusk!"

"Did ya run?"

"Yes, I ran! I was scared when the man began to yell that I had shot a man! Wouldn't you have run, Dink!"

"Were dere fingerprints"

"No!"

It did appear that Flagler was still frightened, even as he told the story. Then I stepped in! I had to know for sure if he was my father, regardless of his mental agitation.

"Mr. Flagler, can I ask you a question, which seems to be totally out of place and off the subject here at this point?"

He looked at me and was somewhat puzzled, but agreed to take the question.

"Do you say now that you are or that you are not my father?" I proceeded with some caution and sensitivity.

He dropped his head, but then replied.

"I am your father. When I said I wasn't when we were together last time, it was to protect you and your mother! I am your father."

"Did you know that Barwell had given up his claim to be my father after you left town?" I said, as I hit him with what appeared to be a shocker.

"What?" he offered, as he seemed to analyze that thought. "Then who did he say I am?" he asked.

"He claimed you were the real Ira Pointer!"

This news of Barwell's admission appeared to be totally new to him.

"Can I ask another question about whether or not you are my father?" I politely asked.

"Certainly! There is nothing to hide now and nothing to fear!"

"Did you ever write a book when you were a young preacher!" I asked, waiting to catch another imposter. His answer did surprise me.

"Yes, I wrote a book on eschatology. I set forth a premillennial view of the coming of Christ. I had charts and everything in it. I analyzed Daniel, Matthew 24, the book of Revelation, and many of the themes of the coming of Christ, including the Antichrist, the kingdom, the pre-trib rapture, and even more."

"Can you tell me what a preterist is?" I asked again.

"Well, preterism was not very popular back in those days, but a preterist is one who believes that a good bit of the book of Revelation was fulfilled at the fall of the city of Jerusualem in 70 AD!" he offered without a flinch.

"Are you aware of a secular historian who spoke in his writings of the fall of Jerusalem also?" I asked, thinking he might stumble on this question.

"Sure, it was Josephus!"

I looked at Dink, and he looked at me. Usually I can read suspicion in Dink's face. But there was only amazement.

Then Dink spoke, still shaking his head.

"Well, Preacha! Yer mother's certainty, (his ex-wife, who ought to know Ira Pointer), and now dis knowledge of Ira Poitner's book, oughta convince ya dat he's da real thing!"

I didn't mean to be obstinate or stubborn, but I needed a few more hours to analyze this! I was not ready to embrace William Flagler as my father!

Then a strange sensation came over me as I had to admit the possibility that sitting across from me right now was the real Ira Pointer, my father. It was not the sense of joy and elation that I had longed for, and even anticipated, or expected in my dreams for so many years, even those years I had cried myself to sleep longing to know him! It was an emptiness, and I wondered why! What was wrong! Wouldn't anyone be elated to find his father?

But then another thought came to me. A father is not simply one who impregnates your mother, and then deserts you, never to be seen again until you're thirty years old! A father is one who loves you, who teaches you, who forms and shapes your character, who lovingly disciplines you, who stays with you through thick and thin, who plays ball with you, who teaches you respect for authority, who shows you the importance and value of work, who builds within you perseverance, who models Biblical values before you, and who is always there for you when needed.

I had to conclude that this man was not my father, nor could he ever be my father. I wondered what the big deal was in our day for people to search for someone, who had never earned the right to be called mother or father to them. Yea, to search for people who had given up that right to be called father or mother early in their lives to pursue their own selfish goals, and then return later in life perhaps for the same reason.

Was that to say I had no forgiveness for William Flagler, if he really was Ira Pointer? No, I did forgive him, yet I understood that he could never be my father, for he had forfeited that right when he left me thirty years ago.

Was that to say he and I could not have a friendship in the years to come? No, there could be a friendship, but never a father and a son relationship, for that required years together, as a boy and a man saw their lives entwining together in love and understanding. Yes, that required a man taking the responsibility which was his to be the loving authority over a tender child, pouring his life into him, until in later days he could turn the young boy loose, knowing that his labor and love of those formative years had shaped a life which would continue on the steadfast pathway of righteousness and godliness.

I felt sorry for myself at this moment for never having had such a father, but I felt more sorrow for Ira Pointer, if that was who Flagler was, for having missed that joy and privilege as well---an opportunity which could not be fulfilled now as he sat in a jail cell, or in the future whether he was in or out of jail, after thirty years of a wasted and fleshly life of selfish indulgence.

I tried to explain all of this to Flagler, and he sat there with a studious look on his face. What I was saying seemed to make sense to him, as I saw a tear slipping down his cheek I began to cry, and then Dink stepped forward to witness to him about Christ.

We left the jail that night still uncertain of the claim of William Flagler. Time would tell if the prisoner was Ira Pointer or William Flagler!

I rejoiced for I had peace, a peace I had never possessed in this area, for I had come to see that my search through the years was a false search, which could never be fulfilled. It was true that I could never find a father, even if he was alive today. I had missed that opportunity, as had my father, whoever he was.

I had found my birth mother and we were building a relationship but even in that relationship, we could never recover the lost years of the entwining of our hearts. I also had found a man, who claimed to be my father, but again, the lost years could never be resurrected to live again. In a clear way, my mother's situation was different, for she had lost her son through no fault of her own, whereas my father had willingly forfeited his privilege of fatherhood.

As I turned out the light back at our hotel, and crawled into bed to the snoring of Dink, I realized that one positive did come out of all of this. I could hardly wait to get home to be a father to my son! My heart wept again, though, as I was aware of Dink's snoring, and of the fact that his son was still missing.[1] And probably dead! And through no fault of his own!

---

[1]See Richard P. Belcher, *A Journey in Providence* (Richbarry Press, 1999).

31

The Post Mil View of Matthew 24?

I awakened the next morning long before Dink began to stir. During my time of devotions, I was convicted of my attitude the previous evening. It was incorrect of me to conclude that every search for one's birth parents was foolish, though it seems clear, that this conclusion was true in some cases. Part of the problem is that one can never know the result of such a search. It could be a very joyous experience, or it could be a devastating pursuit, as it seems mine had become. Who could possibly know the end and results, when one walks into a dark tunnel of uncertainty?

I took up my study on <u>Matthew 24</u> once again, and since I had dealt with the pre-mill views of that chapter, I turned to a <u>post-mill conviction</u>.

A Post-millennial View of Matthew 24[1]

<u>Introduction to the Post Mil view of Matthew 24</u>
The preceding chapter gives us the context of Chapter 24 as it tells us of Jesus' pronouncement of the coming judgment on the Jewish nation because of their rejection of their Messiah.

<u>Key to the entire chapter is verse 34 where Jesus says</u>:
This generation shall not pass, till all these things be fulfilled.

Explanation of the key verse:

Many other verses show that this is a reference to the generation of Jews to whom Christ was speaking (see Matthew 11:16; 12:41-42, 45; 25:36). Thus all the things Jesus' speaks of in this chapter shall come to pass before the present generation of people to whom He spoke passed away.

Verses 1-3

Christ speaks to His disciples telling them in this context and in reference to the temple that not one stone shall be left upon another, which shall not be torn down (before the generation of His day passes away).

The disciples response is in the form of inquiry, asking, "Tell us, when shall these things be? And what shall be the sign of Thy coming, and of the end of the age?"

The interpreter must remember that these verses (according to the context and the key verse noted above) is speaking of events which must come to pass before the present generation of Christ's day passes away.

Verses 4-35

Since this is a description of events which must come to pass before the passing of the generation of Christ's day, to what event or events of history do they refer?

1. They do not refer to the Second Coming at the end of this age because that event exceeds far past the time of the generation of Christ's day.

2. They do refer to the coming of Christ in power to judge the Jewish nation at the time of the fall of Jerusalem in 70 AD to Titus and the Roman armies.

a. *False Christs, wars and rumors of wars   4-6*

Scripture and history records a number of false Christs and wars (see I John 2:18 and Josephus)

b. *Famines, pestilence and earthquakes   7*

These too are recorded in history and Scripture.

c. *Persecution, and martyrdom, and betrayal, and false prophets and cooling of love   9-12*

These again are recorded in Scripture.

d. *A gospel witness goes out to all the world of that day.   14*

See Romans 10:18 and Colossians 1:6 and 23.

e. *The abomination of desolation and the flight of the believers   15-21*

See Luke 21:20 as it tells of the surrounding of Jerusalem with armies, and the statement that its desolation is near.   See the record of history which tells us that there was a fleeing of Jews from Jerusalem just prior to the fall of Jerusalem, due to a brief withdrawal of the Roman army from the area. Also, history tells of the Roman army entering the temple to set up their pagan signs and to offer pagan sacrifices upon the altar, just before fulfilling Christ's prophecy of the temple being torn down stone upon stone.

f. Great Tribulation 21-22

This is the horrible time prior to and at the time of destruction of Jerusalem and of the temple, along with many of its inhabitants. The writings of Josephus tell us this was a horrible hour.

g. False Christs and False Prophets 23-26

Christ will not come back visibly at this time, but only in judgment. Therefore, during this period His disciples must not be fooled by the false claims of false christs and false prophets.

h. Rapid Destruction at the Judgment Coming of Christ 27-28

Jerusalem may be seiged for a number of months, but when she falls and is destroyed, it will be with a rapidity as symbolized in the lightening. Again, it will be a horrible time, with dead bodies abounding.

i. Cataclysmic Eruptions in the Heavens 29

The smiting of the sun, moon and stars is common apocalyptic language to describe a time of judgment, though it is symbolic rather than literal (see Isaiah 13:10; 34:4-5; Ezekiel 32:7; and Amos 8:9).

j. *The Sign of the Son of Man in Heaven   30*

The Son of Man does not appear in the heavens, but the sign of the Son of Man appears in the heavens. Exactly what that sign is, we are not told, but men shall see the sign and will view the sign as evidence of His power and glory. The coming of this hour is His coming in judgment upon Jerusalem. This is a sign that the Son of man reigns in heaven.

k. *The Gathering of the Elect   31*

This verse speaks of the fact that the deliverance of all the elect throughout the world from sin is at hand, as the gospel goes forth to call them out.

l. *The Parable of the Budding Fig Tree   32-35*

This carries the reader back to the key verse noted above, which indicates that these events are not far in the future, but are at hand. When a fig tree puts forth its leaves, one knows the summer is near (31). So likewise, when the Jew at that time saw the above events beginning to unfold, he was to know that the fall of Jerusalem was near (32). And the generation Christ addresses will not pass away till all of these things are fulfilled (33). A further guarantee is added, as Christ notes that heaven and earth shall pass away, but His word shall not pass away.

Summary

Thus this whole section of Matthew 24 deals with the fall of Jerusalem in 70 AD to Titus and the Roman army.

About this time Dink began to move. He kept murmuring as he woke up, "I can't believe dat I slept dis late!" But then he would turn over and sleep some more.

I really didn't mind, as it was still fairly early, and I was still meditating on various other views of Bible prophecy. But then he came out of the bed, when the phone rang loudly, almost right in his ear. As he covered his head up in a pillow, I answered it.

"Preacher Pointer?" the voice inquired, in a hushed manner.

I couldn't imagine who would call me that way out here in Texas, unless it was a long distance call.

"Yes, this is Pastor Ira Pointer!" I offered. But I wasn't prepared for what came next!

"This is Samuel Barwell! You've got to help me!" he stated with apparent nervousness in his voice.

"Help you? Where are you? I thought you were dead!" I thought out loud, as Dink came awake on that one.

"I had just as well have been dead, in light of what I've been through. Please! I haven't got much time! Please come to 839 Pier St. I'll be hiding, but when I see you, I'll signal you to come to me!"

Then he was gone! No explanations! No guarantees of our safety. No number to call him back. Just an address and a plea for help.

By now Dink was wide awake, and his mind and mouth were going the usual ninety miles an hour.

"Preacha, der's sometin' fishy here! We gotta weigh da options before we goes down der! It sound like an ambush ta me!"

"But who would ambush us?" I asked.

"I dunno! But it stinks and I can smell it from here!"

"Okay, what are our options?" I asked, since he had brought the subject to our attention.

"Call da police an let dem go wid us! Or talk ta Flagler before we goes. Or don't go an' den wait an' see what he does! Or go down der alone an' see what happens!"

We decided to go to the police station and see if William Flagler knew anything about this latest development. But when we got there, he had been released by the police. They told us Samuel Barwell had come to the police station during the night, and they could not hold Flagler any longer, since there was no crime. When I asked if they left together or alone, no one knew.

So our options were beginning to fad. The police would not go with us to meet Barwell, since they had no interest in him. We couldn't talk to Flagler, because he was now out of jail and had left no message for us. The choice was either not to go or to go alone! Not much of a choice!

---

[1]See Keith A. Mathison, *Postmillennialism: An Eschatology of Hope* (Presbyterian and Reformed Publishing Company, 1999), pp. 111-115 and J. Marcellus Kik, *An Eschatology of Victory* (Presbyterian and Reformed Publishing Company, 1971) pp. 53-157 for excellent discussions of a post-mil view of Matthew 24.

32

Did You Know My Real Father?

I decided we needed to go, and Dink was willing to accompany me. Who would be better to go with me than Dink? The convincing thought to go was the uncertainty of who these guys were, and what their intentions were, and the potential of further danger to me, my family, and my mother. She for some reason seemed to be their target. Could it be that they were in cahoots together after all, and we would never be able to rest, until the matter was settled?

We made our way in our rented car to a real seedy and apparently deserted part of town down on the gulf. It was clear this area previously had been a thriving beehive of maritime activity, but now the buildings were dilapidated and beyond repair. I wondered why the city had not just bulldozed the whole mess down and allowed something else to develop there. The very appearance of the area was frightening because of its empty deserted atmosphere. Some one could assault you in broad daylight in the middle of any street, and no one would ever hear your cries for help!

We found the address which Barwell had given us and stopped to wait for someone to appear from the myriad of buildings around us. I noticed that by my watch, we were a few minutes early. The uncertainty of the hour increased my heartbeat and put me on edge as we waited. Dink was in the driver's seat, and I could tell he was tense also and ready to act depending on the situation. His eyes kept scanning the landscape of buildings in front of us, on the side of us, and even to the back of us on the rear view mirror. The hour of our appointment arrived, and still no one appeared.

Then from the closest building, which was also the most rickety and decaying building, William Flagler appeared, and he wasn't in his bow tie and plaid coat!

"Its Flagler and not Barwell!" I noted to Dink, thinking out loud again. "What do you make of that?"

"Well, it sure looks now like we been stung. Dose guys has been workin' tagether all along!"

Dink started the engine in anticipation of getting out of there and quick. Flagler countered by holding his hands up and then by opening his coat to show he had no weapon. We waited as he walked toward us. Dink slid the window down a couple of inches so he could hear what Flagler had to say, as he also inched the gear shift into drive.

"Easy, boys!" Flagler spoke. I couldn't tell whether it was a warning or just a greeting.

"No need to drive off. If you did you would just have to come back!" he stated with an arrogance and hardness I had not seen from him previously. It seemed clear that the charade and masquerade of being Ira Pointer was over.

"We had you guys going there, didn't we!" he chortled gloatingly. "This has got to go down as one of our best stings!"

"I told ya dis was a sting and dey was both in on it!" Dink whispered to me, hardly moving his lips, and with his eyes still on Flagler.

"Come on boys, get out. We're going to entertain you for a little while!" Flagler offered.

"Why should we get outta dis car? You got no weapon, an we could just roar outta here!" Dink countered.

"I told you that you would be back!" Flagler stated, still flashing an evil smile.

"What would bring us back ta dis place?" Dink asked.

Then Flagler leaned over so I could see him clearly at the driver's window, and replied, "We've got Pointer's mother!"

"Where?" Dink and I both barked out.

"And why?" I added before he could answer.

"Well, let's say that she is the object of our sting, well, at least her money is. We want a share of it!"

"You mean you have kidnapped her, and now you want a ransom fee to release her?" I asked, stating what seemed the obvious.

"Yes, and now we've got you guys too! And we don't want you guys running around loose to botch up the ransom negotiations and the eventual exchange of the money! So come on, get out of the car---now!!" he stated emphatically without even the evil smile on his face.

"How does we know ya got her?" Dink asked.

"How does ya know we ain't?" Flagler shot back, mocking Dink's pattern of speech, with a Richard Widmark smile and smart-aleck smirk added.

"Preacha, we aint't got much choice!" Dink noted. "If we roar outta here, and dey got her, it could go bad on her. Dese guys play rough, and I tink we can believe dem when dey say theys got her!"

"I think you're right, Dink!" I admitted with sorrow

Dink shut off the engine, and we got out of the car. When we did, several others came out of the decaying woodwork of the old buildings with guns, including a guy with what looked to me to be a bazooka! When I called it a bazooka, I was corrected by Dink. He informed me that it was a L.A.W (Light Anti-tank Weapon), and that the bazooka had not been manufactured for over thirty years! The L.A.W. was a disposable weapon with one rocket in it.

Then a truck entered the street from another building down the way. It stopped in front of us, and the back of it opened, and there was Barwell, laughing in glee, and exclaiming, "Now the fun starts!"

He ordered us into the truck with him, and the door was closed, and the truck began to move. There was a light on in the back as we sat on the floor, but since it was an enclosed bed, we could not see out at all. We had no idea where they were taking us.

The ride did give us a chance to pick the brain of our captor. He informed us that the whole thing was a sting to lure us to Texas where they could culminate the kidnapping and get a large ransom. The entire story they told, as each one of them came separately to our city originally, was part of the sting. All the switching of claims and the seeking to establish Flagler as my father, were planned and perfected as the sting was carried out. He even rattled off all the areas of eschatology that I had quizzed him about, showing he could have answered that question, if he had chosen. Plus, the claim of his murder, and the arrest of Flagler, were staged to lure us to Texas. All of this was even a sting on the police. Even the eyewitness was one of their men. They knew the police could not keep Flagler, when Barwell was obviously alive. Everything was a sting.

Dink looked at me and repeated his conviction, "Preacha, I told ya so from da beginning.'"

I must admit as I rode along and thought about it, that I was extremely glad that neither one of these guys was my father!

That left me with just one more question for Barwell.

"Did either of you guys ever know my real father?"

33

Who Are the Real Kidnap Victims?

When I asked that question, concerning Barwell and Flagler knowing my father, I didn't expect a positive answer. But I hoped they might add more to the puzzle of who he was, and where we might find him today.

Their answer was similar to what they had maintained when first visiting us in our city, as they sought to kick off the sting against us. They had known my father in prison, almost immediately after he had changed his identity. He shared everything about his past with them, including his wife and son, and even where they were living. He also taught them the Bible. Time in prison hangs heavy, so why not study the Bible, and even theology, especially Bible prophecy? Maybe it could be helpful to them one day in one of their future scams.

Flagler and Barwell had been put in jail due to a failure in one of their stings. They said my father even had a copy of his book, and they all read it together and discussed it in great depth. That is why either one of them could have answered my questions on eschatology.

Then I asked them about my father's present whereabouts, and they admitted they knew nothing. He had broken with them after several scams, after getting out of prison, and then he disappeared. He seems to have done what he had done previously---change his identity again, and then he virtually disappeared into thin air. They never saw him again after that, but they had kept up with me and my mother---our whereabouts and status. They had tried to find him also, but it was a dead-end to them, just as his trail had been to us.

I must admit, this information added something to our knowledge. We had been looking for a man, who had changed his identification not just once, but twice! I wondered if that would help or hinder Mack's investigative reporters---if we ever got out of this to tell them?

When I asked them if they knew why he had left them and changed his identity a second time, they weren't sure. But they did say it might have had something to do with being tired of this way of life, and of a desire to go back into the ministry.

I looked at Dink, and said, "The search doesn't get any easier, does it?"

He nodded but gave no answer. It was clear to me, though probably not to them, that Dink was in deep study about our situation and what we might expect next.

After a couple hours of riding, the truck stopped. We heard doors opening, and then closing, after the truck advanced a little further. When the door was opened, we stepped out into a sealed garage area. They led us to a room, and we were made comfortable, and told that when they had received the ransom money, they would let us go.

Not knowing whether or not the room was bugged, we spoke in whispers. I asked Dink what he made of all of this.

"Well, Preacha, first, I don't tink dey gots yer mother! It would be too hard ta get her money as ransom fer her wid her as da kidnap victim. She's got all da money, and she controls da money, so why kidnap her to get her money fer her!" he explained.

"Second," he continued, "we'se da kidnap victims, and deys gonna use us ta get ransom money from her ta get us back!"

I had to admit, he had two good points.

"Third, deys wantin' to keep us from tryin' ta escape by tellin' us dat deys got her and dat she's in danger, if we'se try ta escape. Dats da way dey use ta try ta make us be good boys and stay here?"

I had to admit again, another good point. I also had to admire the way Dink's mind analyzed these criminals' methods! But why not, in light of his past criminal record?

"Then what do we do?" I asked, somewhat ashamed of my ignorance at this point.

"Preacha, we can escape at any time we wants ta---dat is, if we gets da chance, cause yer mother ain't in no danger!" he offered.

"But can we take the chance that they might really have her, and that it would be very difficult for her if we escaped?" I countered. "Don't you remember, they said that if we had left, we would have come back? Wouldn't that be when we learned she was in danger?"

"Preacha, don't ya remember da L.A.W?" he reminded me. "Dat was der for a purpose---to use if we tried to escape in the car!" he said shockingly.

"You don't mean it!" I spoke with some volume, forgetting that the place might be bugged.

Dink shushed me, as silently as he could!

"Preacha, unless we escape sometime during all dis, we ain't never gonna get out alive!" he predicted.

"Wow!" I said, using a word more common to Dink's mode of expression. "What's our escape plan?" I asked, knowing he was my lifeline, humanly speaking, at this moment.

"I dunno, Preacha. I'm studyin' dat right now! We might have ta play it by ear, and react when dey act, if we can't find no plan before den!"

About that time the door opened, and Flagler came in with another guy.

"I thought you might like to have your things from the hotel!" he said, as they threw down our small bags before us. "Don't ever say that old William Flagler doesn't take care of his 'son' and his sidekick!" he said in his Richard Widmark voice and smile.

I couldn't tell if that was the real Flagler, or just an act. But I guarantee you, I did rejoice, because there were my books and notes on prophecy! That meant more to me than my clothing! I'm not sure Dink was happy about it, though. He didn't seem to be as interested in eschatology as he had been in my previous studies. He kept telling me that I was going to burn my brain out on all that prophecy stuff. He said he was ready for Jesus' coming, and didn't want to be bothered with the details.

I was satisfied at this moment for his brain to figure out a way for us to escape! I couldn't help but admire Dink--- he was a sincere soul, with a keen street-smart mind, and a brave heart! God had been not only gracious when He saved Dink, but also gracious to give him to me as a friend.

We went to sleep that night, after prayer, and I felt even greater loneliness, as I heard the whistle of a train somewhere outside in the distance.

34

The A-Mil View of Matthew 24?

As previously, I woke up before Dink the next morning. Since there were no windows in our room, I turned on a dim light so I could study Matthew 24 from an a-mil position. I summarized that view from a commentary I had brought with me.[1]

An A-mil View of Matthew 24

1. The material in this chapter and in the following chapter is two-fold in its reference. Some of it refers to the fall of Jerusalem in 70 AD, and some of it refers to events further in the future, even the second coming of Christ at the end of the age (see 24:14, 29-31, and 25:6, 31-46).

2. The material in this chapter weaves together these two important events of the history of the people of God, and, the first, the fall of Jerusalem, is a type or picture of the final tribulation at the end of this age.

3. The material in this chapter cannot be limited to the first of these momentous events, that is, the fall of Jerusalem alone, and not to the Second Coming at the end of the age for clear reasons:

a. *If that be the case, then Jesus never answered the disciples' question, "What shall be the sign of Thy coming, and of the end of this age."*

b. *Matthew 24 cannot be divorced from Matthew 25. If Matthew 24:29-31 refers only to the fall of Jerusalem, and not to the Second Coming of Christ, then that must be true also of chapter 25:31-46, as there is a parallel between them. In both chapters:*

   1) The Son of man appears in great glory.

   2) The people (His elect) are gathered before Him.

   3) Thus when 25:46 clearly indicates that the end of the age has been reached, then the content of both sections must refer to the end of the age, in light of the clear parallel already seen.

I then added a quotation from the author mentioned in the first footnote:

It is not claimed, of course, that any exegete is able completely to untangle what is here intertwined, so as to indicate accurately for each individual passage just how much refers to Jerusalem's fall, and how much to the great tribulation and the second coming.[2]

I then made a note that the reader, who was interested in seeing how Hendriksen untangled the subject matter, should pursue the matter further in his commentary.

I also noted that it was clear that the a-mil view did see a coming time of tribulation on the earth just prior to the Second Coming of Christ.

I also noted that both the pre-mil and the a-mil see a time of tribulation prior to the Second Coming of Christ, whereas, the post-mill believes the age will end with the coming of Christ to a Christianized world.

After breakfast, about the time Dink and I had settled down to think more of the possibilities of escape, we were interrupted by Flagler again.

"Boys, you're free to go! We don't need you any more, because we've got the money---a cool two mil!"

"Already?" I said with some skepticism, thinking, you can't trust a scam-man to tell you the truth.

"Yep, we had men in place, and after we picked you guys up yesterday, it only took a short time to get the dough!" he explained. "So come on, gather up your things. You're going home!!"

As he left the room, I looked at Dink shaking my head.

"You'se right, Preacha! Dey may have da dough, but we ain't goin home! We'se goin ta see da Lord, which would be nice, mind you. But I ain't sure its His time yet."

"What do we do?" I asked somewhat fearfully.

"We'se got to react to how dey act, an trust da Lord ta give us a time and a place to bust loose!" he explained.

"But what if they just shoot us now! We'll have no chance to react to that! What if they hit this place with a rocket? We're no match for a rocket?"

"Well, den we'll see Jesus pretty quick!"

The door opened again, and they conducted us back to the truck, put us in it, and locked the door from the outside. There was only one other opening into the internal portion of the truck where we were captives, and that was a door at the top, which was padlocked from the inside. Dink went to work immediately, pulling from his boot (he always wore boots), some kind of foreign knife with a hundred or so little tools that sprang out of it. That's the first time I had ever seen it in all the time we had spent together. Standing on my shoulders, he began trying to pick the lock. And presto! Just as the truck began to move, the lock came open.

"Now what?" I asked.

It's a wonder Dink didn't get tired of my questions. He did all the thinking as to how to get us out, and then did all the work to get us free, and all I could do was stand around and ask questions.

"Follow me, Preacha! Do just as I do! Don't let yer arms hang over da edge of da truck, or da rear view mirror can pick you up. An be as quiet as a dead church mouse! And don't bring yer briefcase---we'se travelin' light!"

With those words he jumped, grabbed the roof of the truck, and pulled himself up through the opening onto the top of the truck. I followed, but must admit, I was not as smooth, nor did I evidence his skilled dexterity. All this with the truck going 45-50 miles an hour---and no books!.

I followed him as he slid quietly across the top of the truck to the rear, and started down the ladder to the back bumper, where he stood, hanging on, while I came down to stand beside him. As we swung and bounced in the breeze, he explained our next move.

"Preacha, dis vehicle has got ta slow down fer sumptin' sometime. When it does, we is going off. As soon as ya hit da ground, lie down flat. Don't go runnin' off into da weeds. Der ain't no traffic behind us, so ders no danger of getting' run over by another vehicle. A runnin' figure is easier to pick up in da rear view mirror dan a body layin' flat on the road straight back from a car. Got it?"

I nodded yes, and wondered what in the world we were going to do after we got off, but there was no time to ask, as we began slowing down for something.

When the "vehicle," as Dink liked to call it, almost stopped, we were off. I hit the cement highway pretty hard, and went down, but by no choice of my own. So I just stayed there, as the truck roared its engine and moved on. When they were out of sight, Dink and I hit the ditch to hide. I couldn't wait to hear his plan for our next move!

"Well, what now?" I asked.

"Preacha, we got about twenty minutes ta catch our train!" he answered in all seriousness.

"What train?" I asked, in the same serious spirit.

"I don't know, but if my calculations are correct, it'll be comin' in about twenty minutes on a track to da north!" he explained. "Doncha remember da train we heard all day yesterday?" he asked.

"Wow!" I gasped. "I had heard it once, in the lonely hours at bedtime. Did you hear it more than that?"

"Preacha, dat train ran once an hour---at about fifteen minutes past da hour. I don't know which way it was goin,' but I know which way it was from da place we were staying---north."

"But how did you know which way was north in the place where we stayed?" I asked.

"I noted dat as we came out! I knew which direction da noise came from, and I remembered as we came to da truck in dat garage, or whatever it was. Even though da windows was covered, I could see where da sun was. So I took note a dat, an' den I remembered da direction of da train, an' bingo---da train's to da north. Dat ain't so hard, is it?"

"But why did you note that?" I asked mystified.

"I noted a lotta tings---anyting dat might help us escape! An' dat was one of dem! Come on, Preacha! We gotta get movin' and find dat railroad track. Ya don't want ta miss dis train, do ya? Besides, dose guys might come back lookin' fer us."

"But how are we going to get on a moving train?" I asked, wondering if I was beginning to sound like a tenderfoot.

"Just opposite of how ya got off of da truck!" Dink said with a smile. "On one of dem, ya turn loose, and on da other one, ya just grab and hang on an' pull yerself up!"

"But don't you have to run in the process?" I asked again.

"Yeah, sure. Der may be a little jerk as ya run and grab on to a train movin' faster dan youse runnin.' But da pain don't last long!"

I thought to myself, I had rather be studying eschatology---the last days---rather than experiencing what might be my last day!. If it was my last day before His coming, come quickly, Lord Jesus!

I was interrupted in my musings of self-pity by Dink, as he hit the ground and beckoned me to do the same. I looked back towards the road, which was several hundred yards away by now, and there was the truck coming back. They were trying to figure out where they had lost us.

Now we had to dodge a truck and catch a train!

---

[1]William Hendrikson, *New Testament Commentary: Exposition of the Gospel according to Matthew* (Baker Book House, 1989, tenth printing), p. 846ff.

[2]Ibid., pp. 847-48.

35

Where Do I Look Now?

As we moved to the north, we stayed as low to the ground as possible. And sure enough, in about fifteen minutes we came to the railroad track! Now, would the train accommodate us and be on time?

We waited, but the train was nowhere to be found. First, it was five minutes, and then ten minutes past the time Dink said it was due. Fortunately, we hadn't seen our pursuers since the first sighting at the road. By now, though, we were several miles north of that road.

Then Dink turned and said, "There it is, Preacha!"

I looked and saw nothing.

"Naw, I don't mean I see it. I hear it. Dontcha hear da whistle, Preacha?" he asked.

I marveled again at the sensitivity of his senses---all of them---as I heard nothing! Then I heard it. In a few minutes, we saw it, and we began to move to get into position to jump it.

"Preacha, we gets on dat train first, and den we try ta find an empty box car. If we can't find one, we just ride on da top to da first stop, where we den find da police!"

As the train approached us, I noticed that it was slowing down some, due to a slight grade it was climbing. God's providence!! Dink looked at me and gave me the thumbs up sign as he noticed the same. Knowing the train was a long one, we let the engine move past us, and then the race began! We came out of the Texas brush like scared jackrabbits. I don't think I have ever run as fast in my life, and soon I was breathing heavily.

I remembered a guy in high school, who I used to watch during the district and state track meets, as I was pole vaulting. He ran the mile. As I stood at the end of the runway waiting to vault one day, he passed by at the beginning of the final curve, and I heard him say, "Come on legs! Let's go!" Its strange what one remembers from the past in unique situations, as they are unfolding with great rapidity. I found myself saying the same thing to my legs! And they went!

Dink grabbed the train first, and swung aboard. I grabbed the next ladder, which seemed as if it was going to whiz past me, and I hung on for dear life! Again, I wasn't as agile as Dink, and so I found myself swinging and fighting to pull up and plant my feet on the lower rung. Finally, I was firmly planted on the ladder, both hands and both feet in place, and I just rested there for a few minutes, before climbing to the top of the train.

By then Dink had made his way to help me, if I needed it. We stretched ourselves out on the top of the train, and I then noticed that my lungs were a ball of fire, and I was about to breath my insides out, as I gulped for every breath of air. I really feared the possibility of a heart attack! I didn't even have the strength to try to find that empty box car.

I don't know how long we agonized prostrate on the top of the train, but finally, we began to feel refreshed. But then we noticed something! The train track and the highway had converged and were now running parallel, rather than being several miles apart. And there on the highway, was the truck! They had found us! And a bullet or two whizzed past our heads!

Then I noticed that the train was picking up speed, while the truck was struggling to keep up with us! Then they shot ahead of us, and began to gain on the engine.

"What are they doing?" I asked Dink.

He didn't answer at first, and then he saw it.

"Preacha, deys tryin' ta beat da train to da next crossin'. Dey must figure, fer some reason, dat if da train beats dem ta da crossin' dat we will get away."

Since they were't shooting at us any more, Dink and I sat up to watch the surprising events unfolding before our eyes. And sure enough, Dink was right. The truck gained speed to where it was in an even race with the engine, and then it began to edge ahead. Then we saw the crucial crossing in the distance, around the curve, where the road did cross over the tracks.

Being so far back on the train, we couldn't judge the distance with perfection. Thus when the truck left our sight as it sought to cross in front of the train, we felt the engineer brake the train, which almost threw us off. Still we kept looking for the truck to come out on the other side of the tracks. But it never did. In fact, as we shot past the crossing, we saw the results of what had to have been a massive collision between the two. There were pieces of metal, and even some bodies strewn hither and yon as we continued down the tracks, as the engineer sought to bring the train to a stop.

It seemed clear that Flagler and Barwell and their henchmen in the truck were dead! Though I meant no disrespect to the dead, I wondered also about my eschatology notes and the two million dollars, which had been on the truck.

When the train stopped, Dink and I embarked and walked back down the tracks towards the crossing. Dink was on one side of the train, and I was on the other side, as we also surveyed the landscape for any of our belongings, as well as the money.

Soon the police were there, and though they didn't seem to believe us at first, as we told our story, all the contacts we gave them to make, as well as the evidence at the scene of the crash, verified our testimony. They told us that Barwell and Flagler were trying to beat the train, because they knew they would have no chance to catch us if they didn't. It seems the train track and the road go to the same town, where the train always stops, but the tracks are direct, and the road is about twenty miles further, as it winds through the Texas brush.

They did find my notes, one of the only things in the crash that had remained in one piece, thanks to the Lord's providence, and my good old gorilla-jump-up-and-down-on-it-you-cannot-hurt-it-briefcase. The two million dollars was strewn all over the place, but it too was recovered. And, yes, our captors were all dead! But then so were all our contacts to my father's past!

When we arrived home, I found a message from Mack Turnover, telling me that neither Flagler nor Barwell were my father, but they were con men. I smiled as I read his message! I thought, "Thanks for telling me what I already knew and had learned the hard way." I had no idea where to look now.

My thoughts turned once again to my family, my church, and my sermon preparation. My personal historical search was as puzzling at this moment, so it seemed, as Biblical eschatology! The great difference was, that in Biblical eschatology I had a revelation from God to follow in my search. Maybe I needed something like that in my search for my father---at least a clue of some kind.

36

The Pre-Mil View of Daniel 9?

After a few days at home with the opportunity for things to get back to normal, my mind turned again to my eschatological search. I decided that the next key passage of Scripture to pursue was Daniel 9. It seemed to be a key to the question of a literal period of tribulation for Israel in the last days of the history of this age.

The Pre-mil View of Daniel 9[1]

Verse 24---The whole prophecy is presented in one verse

Seventy weeks are determined upon thy people and upon thy holy city, to finish transgression, and to make an end of sins, and to make reconciliation for iniquity, and to bring in everlasting righteousness, and to seal up the vision and prophecy, and to anoint the most Holy.

1. The seventy weeks are to be seen as seventy periods of seven years, making the total a period of 490 years.

2. These 490 years (70 weeks X 7 years each) is a period which has to do with the nation of Israel (thy people) and upon God's holy city (Jerusalem).

3. These 490 years will bring some clear results concerning Israel and the city of Jerusalem:

    a) to finish transgression
    b) to make an end of sins
    c) to make reconciliation for iniquity
    d) to bring in everlasting righteousness
    e) to seal up the vision and prophecy
    f) to anoint the most Holy.

Verse 25---The period of sixty-nine sevens is described.

Know therefore and understand that from the going forth of the commandment to restore and to build Jerusalem unto the Messiah the Prince shall be seven weeks, and three score and two weeks: the street shall be built again, and the wall, even in troublous times.

1. The beginning of the period of 490 years is the commandment to restore and rebuild Jerusalem. The great question is, when did this begin. Sir Robert Anderson and others have noted that there were several decrees regarding the restoration of Israel from Babylon, but only one that concerned the rebuilding of Jerusalem itself. That one was in the twentieth year of Artaxerxes in 445 BC.[2] Anderson then argues that the ending of the period was the day Christ entered Jerusalem at what is known as His triumphal entry. Whether one agrees with this argument of exactness, the pre-mil would say that the time element is accurate.

2. The period here in verse 25 is divided (the reason for the division is not obvious) into two periods: one of seven weeks (49 years) and one of three score and two weeks or seventy-two weeks, or a total of 69 weeks (483 years).

Verse 26---The events between the sixty-ninth and the seventieth seven is described.

And after threescore and two weeks shall Messiah be cut off, but not for himself; and the people of the prince that shall come shall destroy the city and the sanctuary; and the end thereof shall be with a flood, and unto the end of the war desolations are determined.

1. Thus after the 69 weeks, several events are noted that will take place:

   a) the Messiah will be cut off.
   b) the people of the prince that shall come shall destroy the city of Jerusalem and the sanctuary, that is, the temple. The prince here is the Antichrist, and his people, though he is not on the scene when it takes place, would be the people of the Roman Empire under Titus when he destroyed Jerusalem in 70 AD.

2. The end coming with a flood, etc., would also refer to the destruction of Jerusalem in 70 AD and accompanying events.

Verse 27---The final period of the seventieth seven is described.

And he shall confirm the covenant with many for one week: and in the midst of the week he shall cause the sacrifice and the oblation to cease, and for the overspreading of abominations he shall make it desolate, even until the consummation, and that determined shall be poured upon the desolate.

1. There is a clear separation of the 69 weeks from the final week, or what is known as the seventieth week of Daniel. Thus they will not be fulfilled simultaneously, but there will be a gap between these two periods of time.

2. Note the following events of the final one week period, or the seventieth week of Daniel:

   a) Someone (he---depending on the antecedent of this pronoun) will confirm the covenant with many (probably Israel) for this final one week period. The problem is whether the pronoun finds its antecedent in "Messiah" or in "prince" in verse 26, or even perhaps the Messiah and the prince are the same person. The usual pre-mil view is that they are different, and that the antecedent is the prince, who is the Antichrist. Thus, the Antichrist makes a covenant with Israel for the last seven year period.

   b) The Antichrist during this period will do the following:

      1) he will break his covenant with the Jews in the midst of the week

2) he will cause the sacrifice and the oblation to cease at that time

3) he will bring abominations and desolations for the rest of the period of his rule---the last three and one half years of his seven year tenure.

Conclusion

It is then that the results in verse 24 will be fulfilled:

1. transgressions will be finished
2. an end will be made of sins
3. reconciliation will be made for iniquity
4. everlasting righteousness will be brought in
5. the prophecy and vision will be sealed up
6. the most Holy will be anointed

I leaned back in my chair, after making these notes, to let my mind rest. I still had a few aches and bruises from the train and truck escapade. I had a number of books stacked around me, which I had been using as resource material. My eyes caught a glancing view of the cover of a book I had looked through several times. Then something dawned upon me, which I had never noticed previously--- something that could be a clue in my search for my father!

---

[1]See John F. Walvoord, *Daniel:The Key to Prophetic Revelation* (Moody Press, 1971), pp. 216-232, and Dwight Pentecost, *Things to Come* (Dunham Publishing Company, 1958), pp. 239-250).

[2]Pentecost, p. 246.

37

The A-Mil View of Daniel 9?

That which jarred me in my moment of reverie was the cover of one of the books. I picked it up, and thought to myself that I had seen the chart on that cover in some other book. I opened the pages of the one in my hand, and again, the charts within resembled ones I had seen elsewhere.

Thus I began flipping through each book I had been using, and there it was! The charts in the first book, the one which had raised me from my moment of abstract musing were very much, if not identical, to the charts in the old book I had, which had been authored by my father. Could that be?

I discovered that the content was different, in that my father's book was strictly dispensational pre-mil, while the newer book was an a-mil view point, yet had charts of the several views. All the charts were identical in style and some were identical also in content!

My conclusion was clear! Either the author of the new book was my father, or the author had plagiarized my father's book. But who was this new author? His name was Brandon Phillips, and just as my father had placed his initials into his charts (IP), so this author had placed his initials (BP) in his charts as well. But who was he?

Eagerly I turned to the copyright page to see when this book had been published. The date was 1961! That means, if my father's book had been written in the early fifties, then this book was written ten years later. But again, who was this Brandon Phillips? I determined that I would soon find out! I had another hour or so before things would open up (I was an early riser), so I wanted to finish another of the views on Daniel 9:24-27.

The A-mil View of Daniel 9:24-27[1]

The Setting

    The children of Israel are in the ending days of their captivity in Babylon. Daniel, interceding for the people, asks God what is going to happen next. The answer is given in this ninth chapter, verses 24-27.

The Message

    God has decided something for the future of His people---seventy weeks are determined upon God's people and His holy city.

1. What are the seventy weeks? 24

    The literal meaning is seventy sevens, but this is a symbolical number. They convey an idea of exactness of fulfillment, but not an exactness of the time element.

2. What will happen during this period of time? The author of Daniel gives us three negatives and three positives, all of which take place at the first coming of Christ. 24

    a) Negative one---to put away transgression
    b) Negative two---to make an end of sins
    c) Negative three---to make reconciliation for
        iniquity

Note that all of the negatives have to do with God putting an end to sin, which took place at Christ's first coming.

Note now the positives:

d) to bring in everlasting righteousness
e) to seal up the vision and prophecy---to finish it
f) to anoint the most holy

All of these also refer to Christ and what He did at His first coming.

3. When and how will all this take place?   25-27

Verse 25-26a
25   Know therefore and understand, that from the going forth of the commandment to restore and to build Jerusalem unto the Messiah the Prince shall be seven weeks, and threescore and two weeks: the street shall be built again, and the wall, even in troublous times. 26   And after threescore and two weeks shall the Messiah be cut off, but not for himself...

a) The date to rebuild Jerusalem is difficult to nail down, thus we cannot be literal, but notice the reality that it went forth in the Old Testament period.

b) The Messiah the Prince (the Anointed Prince) is the Messiah, that is, the Lord Jesus Christ.

   c) The weeks are divided into seven, sixty-two, and the final week (see entire context)

The <u>seven weeks</u> cover the time of the rebuilding of the city of Jerusalem and the temple.

The <u>sixty-two weeks</u> cover the time onward to the coming of Christ at His first advent.

<u>Verse 26b</u>
And the people of the prince that shall come shall destroy the city and the sanctuary; and the end thereof shall be with a flood, and unto the end of the war desolations are determined.

This speaks of the destruction of the city of Jerusalem in 70 AD by Titus and the Roman armies.

The <u>final week</u> is very difficult with much disagreement, thus we cover it now under a separate heading.

<u>Verse 27</u>
And he shall confirm the covenant with many for one week; and in the midst of the week he shall cause the sacrifice and the oblation to cease, and for the overspreading of the abominations, he shall make it desolate, even until the consummation, and that determined shall be poured upon the desolate.

The "he" in this verse is not the antichrist, but the Messiah Himself. The best translation is not to make a covenant, but to confirm one. Christ confirmed the covenant that was already in place---the covenant of grace and salvation.

Further, "he" (Christ) made the sacrifices and oblations cease in that he was the anti-type of all the Old Testament types, which ended with His coming. The proof is that there is no temple or sacrifices being offered today. The one final offering has been made, and all others have ceased.

Again, "he" (Christ), for the overspreading of abominations, made it desolate, etc. This is a reference to the desolation which came at the destruction of Jerusalem by Titus and the Roman armies in 70 AD.

Lloyd-Jones summarizes this view as follows:

I see in this section of Daniel a most astounding prophecy of what literally took place over five hundred years later. What a foreview of the gospel! What a marvelous prophecy of God's eternal way of salvation! Daniel, you remember, was troubled. He said: What is going to happen? What will the future be? And here is the answer. He is told what will happen to his nation and to his people. But, thank God, it does not stop at that. He is also told of what God will do in fulfillment of His ancient covenant and promise. He is told about the Messiah, the everlasting righteousness, the atonement, the reconciliation and all the glory of the Christian salvation. It seems to me to be totally unnecessary to introduce a gap between weeks sixty-nine and seventy. Seventy follows on directly from the sixty-nine. These things are in a sequence and they happened in the very sequence taught here.[2]

By the time I finished this outline, I was eager to begin making some phone calls, to see if I could find out who Brandon Phillips was. Surely someone will know who he was or who he is! If I couldn't find out, surely Mack's people could.

I don't know if I could take another crashing dead end!

---

[1]See Martyn Lloyd-Jones, *The Church and the Last Things* (Crossway Books, 1998), pp. 119-129. Lloyd-Jones says his is the view of Edward Young.

[2]Ibid., pp. 135-136.

38

The Post-Mil View of Daniel 9?

As soon as I reached my church office, I tried to get a number for the publishing company listed in the book by Brandon Phillips. The company, at the time the book was written, was located in Nashville, Tennessee, and was called Millennial Publishers. Sure enough, they were still in existence.

I dialed eagerly, and waited impatiently for someone to answer the phone. Finally a voice with a Southern accent answered with a hello, and a "Do ya mind waitin a second?" She never gave me a chance to say yes or no.

Finally, I had a real live voice, and asked if she could give me some information. I concluded it must be a small publishing company, when she answered that I would have to ask someone else, cause all she did was some secretarial work. So I was put on hold again!

Then an older man answered, and he said he would try to help me.

"Did you once publish a book, probably sometime in the sixties, by a Brandon Phillips?" I asked. "It was on the subject of Bible prophecy."

He was a jovial fellow, as he answered with a chuckle, "We could have! All we publish are Bible prophecy books! What did you say the name of the author was?"

"Brandon Phillips!" I stated again.

"Are you looking for that book?" he asked.

"No, I'm looking for the man who wrote it?" I explained.

"Brandon Phillips? Hmmm? Yeah, I remember him! He was that guy who didn't want us to use his real name, and so we published it for him under a pen name. Yeah, Brandon Phillips was this guy's pen name."

"Do you know his real name? Or could you find his real name for me?" I asked, knowing this might be my last hope to find my father.

"Well, I can't say I could tell you off the top of my head, but I can search the records for you. What did you say the name was?"

"Brandon Phillips!" I declared again.

And then I added something to encourage him to call me back.

"By the way, I have a copy of an earlier book very similar to the one you published in content, style and even in the charts used. It was written by a man named Pointer, Ira Pointer!" I informed him.

"Whoa, friend! Are you suggesting that we may have printed a book that was plagiarized by this Brandon Phillips? Wow! That would be serious. You haven't got any intentions of suing us, have you? By the way, who is this Ira Pointer who wrote the first book?"

I told him Ira Pointer was my father, and then I gave him my name and my phone number, and he promised to call me back within a couple of hours, with or without the information. When we ended the conversation, I felt I had made some progress, but didn't get my hope up too high. I had already seen too many doors slammed in my face when I thought one was opening!

Not knowing when he might call, and not wanting to miss the call, I turned to consider the post-mil view of Daniel 9:24-27

The Post-mil View of Daniel 9:24-27[1]

1. Before one can properly interpret this passage, one must understand its covenantal structure.

   a. Daniel is praying concerning Israel's covenant loyalty or, preferably, Israel's covenant disloyalty.

   b. The prayer is answered in the terms of the covenantal Sabbath pattern of seventy weeks.

   c. Daniel 9 is the only chapter in Daniel to use God's unique covenant name---YHWH (see verses 2, 4, 10, 13, 14, 20).

   d. Covenantal redemption is fulfilled in the ministry of Christ, therefore, this passage is about Christ and His work.

2. This section of prophecy is framed in sabbath chronology. That is, it speaks of a time frame in which redemption is to be accomplished.

   a. Seven weeks or literally seven sevens   25
      or 49
   b. Seventy weeks or seventy sevens   25

3. The seventy weeks represent a period of 490 years--- seventy times seven.

   a. Scripture does give guidance for measuring days in terms of years

Genesis 29:27-28	Ezekiel 4:6
Numbers 14:34	Amos 4:4
Deuteronomy 14:28	I Samuel 2:19

4. The interpretation of the prophecy

<u>Verse 24</u>

Seventy weeks are determined for thy people and upon thy holy city, to finish the transgression, and to make an end of sins, and to make reconciliation for iniquity, and to bring in everlasting righteousness, and to seal up the vision and prophecy, and to anoint the Most Holy.

This statement speaks of six results of the first advent of our Lord

a. "To finish transgression" speaks of Israel finishing her sin and transgression against God. This finishing of transgression by Israel occurred during the ministry of Christ, as she rejected God's Son and crucified Him.

b. "To make an end of sins" might be translated better as to seal up their sins, or to reserve their sins for punishment. Because of Israel's treatment of the Messiah, God has reserved punishment for that nation, specifically, the destruction of the temple and city of Jerusalem in 70 AD.

c. To make reconciliation for iniquity speaks of the atonement, for that is the meaning of the

Hebrew word *kaphar*, which is used here. The word means a covering for sin. It speaks clearly of Christ's atoning death, which is the final atonement towards which all the temple ritual pointed.

d. To bring in everlasting righteousness speaks of the fact that Christ's atonement brings in and establishes true righteousness. His work is the objective accomplishment of God's righteousness, not just a subjective appropriation of righteousness.

e. To seal up the vision and prophecy speaks of Christ's life and work whereby he fulfilled and confirmed all the prophecy spoken concerning Him.

f. To anoint the Most Holy speaks of Christ's baptism, at which time God anointed Him with the Holy Spirit, which was introductory to His ministry.

Verses 25-27

25 Know, therefore, and understand that from the going forth of the commandment to restore and to build Jerusalem, unto the Messiah, the Prince, shall be seven weeks, and threescore and two weeks; the street shall be built again, and the wall, even in troublous times. 26 And after threescore and two weeks shall Messiah be cut off, but not for himself; and the people of the prince that shall come shall destroy the city and the sanctuary, and the end of it shall be with a flood, and unto the end of the war desolations are determined. 27 And he shall confirm the covenant with many for one week; and in the midst of the week he shall cause the sacrifice and the oblation to cease, and for the overspreading of abominations he shall make it desolate, even until the consummation, and that determined shall be poured upon the desolate.

a. The time of the seventy weeks begins with the command to restore and to re-build Jerusalem. The fullness of this command was not taken seriously until the middle of the fifth century BC.

b. The first period of seven weeks is set off from the other weeks. These seven weeks or forty-nine years speaks of the successful conclusion of the rebuilding of Jerusalem.

c. The second period of sixty-two weeks then extends from the conclusion of the rebuilding of Jerusalem to the introduction of the Messiah at His anointing at His baptism, when He begins His public ministry, around 26 AD.

d. The second period, which followed the first period, is now followed by specific experiences by the Messiah. This must take place in the seventieth week, for it is after the other two periods.

1) The key event is that the Messiah shall be cut off, which refers to a violent death.

2) The event is stated also as He is the one who confirms a covenant with many for a week. but in the middle of the week, He shall cause the sacrifice and oblation to cease. The covenant spoken of here is the divine covenant of God's redemptive grace. Christ came to confirm the covenant promises, by His death on the cross.

3) This first half of the final seven years speaks of Christ's life and ministry, and His death in the middle of that period is the confirmation of God's covenant promises.

4) The last half of the final seven years speaks of the three and a half years following His death, when the gospel still went out first to the Jews, and then to the Gentiles.

5) The events described in the last part of both verses 26 and 27, referring to abomination and desolation, etc., tell us of the destruction of the city of Jerusalem, which are the consequences of the cutting off of the Messiah. These events are not necessarily within the seventy weeks time period.

Thus the post-mil and the a-mil views would not see a gap between the sixty-nine weeks and the final seventieth week, as would the pre-mil. The events in this section of prophecy, according to the post-mils and a-mils, see these events fulfilled from an Old Testament day (the command to restore Jerusalem) to the death of Christ and a few years beyond to the fall of Jerusalem in 70 AD

The pre-mil would see a large gap between the sixty-nine weeks and the final seventieth week. The first period of sixty-nine weeks ends with the death of Christ, and the final seventieth week, begins the final seven year period just prior to the Second Coming of Christ in power and glory at the end of this age.

When I finished, I went to get a coke, but sure enough, the phone rang. I scurried back into the office, and it was my friend from Millennial Publishers. But he didn't have good news for me!

---

[1]This material is a summary of discussion found in *He Shall Have Dominion* by Kenneth Gentry, Jr., published by Institute for Christian Economics, 1997, pp. 319-331.

39

Can We Summarize All These Views?

"Mr. Pointer! I searched everywhere for the identity of this Brandon Phillips, but I can't find a thing! I guess he did just use this name once, for a pen name, and then faded into the woodwork again. I wonder why a guy would want to write a book, get it published, and not be known as its author?"

"I was afraid of something like this!" I offered. "Either he had a past to hide, or he was plagiarizing the material from someone else!" I added.

"Whoa, there, partner!" he shot back. "We only published a thousand copies of that book, and it went real slow in sales at that. We lost money in the deal!"

"No, I am not blaming you," I declared. "You asked me why a guy would write a book under a pen name, and I just answered you. Did you ever see this Brandon Phillips?" I tried again.

"Yeah, probably so, but I sure don't remember what he looked like. That's been awhile ago, and we get a lot of folks through here in a year's time. Sorry, but I don't think I can help you."

Thus it appeared that I had struck out once again. Then another idea came to me! Maybe the name Brandon Phillips would mean something to my mother. So I got her on the phone, and after the usual greetings, and then some explanation as to her concerning the book I had found, I asked her the question.

"Mother, does the name Brandon Phillips mean anything to you?"

I was shocked by the silence that followed!

"Son, that sure is a name from the past!" she answered finally.

"Then you did or do know a Brandon Phillips?" I pressed again.

"That's a fictitious name your father used to mention, because he never liked the name Ira Pointer. He jokingly said that he should have been given a name like Brandon Phillips, a name with class, and that someday he might change his name to that name."

"So that name does link my father to that book, which was written in the sixties! He published his book with an updated view of his changes in his eschatology under a pen name!" I marveled at the discovery. "But who was he then? And where was he? In Tennessee? And what was he?"

I had to conclude that the discovery of the book had not helped me at all in my quest, unless I was overlooking something in the mix.

I needed some time to think about it, so I turned to my study on eschatology. I concluded that the time had come for some summary of what I had seen.

The Pre-Millennial View (Futurists)

The Millennium
    a literal 1000 years with Christ ruling on this earth
The Second Coming
    a literal return of Christ to this earth
        prior to the millennium

The Book of Revelation
    a book prophesying the future from our perspective
        in chapters 4-22
The 24th Chapter of Matthew
    a presentation of the future for the most part
        as it speaks of a future tribulation period
        and the second coming of Christ
The 9th Chapter of Daniel
    a prophecy of Daniel whereby he sees
        the history of Israel in a period of 490 years
            (70 weeks)
            with part of it being fulfilled
                between Daniel's time
                and the death of Christ
                    (69 weeks or 483 years)
            with the last part being fulfilled
                at the end of this age
                in what is known as the tribulation period
                    as pictured in the seventieth week
                    or seven literal years
        obviously with a lengthy gap
            between the 69 weeks and the 70th week
            or the last 7 year period
The Rapture
    Pre-mils are divided
        as to whether the rapture will take place
            before the tribulation (pre-trib rapture)
                which is the view of the dispensationalists
            or at the end of the tribulation (post-trib rapture)
                which is the view of the Historic Pre-mils
                and the Covenantal Pre-mils

The A-Millennial View (Historicists)

<u>The Millennium</u>
    the 1000 years are a symbolic figure
        thus there will never be an earthly millennium
        and Christ never will rule on this earth
            because He is now ruling in heaven
                from His Davidic throne
<u>The Second Coming</u>
    a literal return of Christ to this earth
        not to rule but set in motion
            all of the final events of history
                which will culminate in the eternal state
<u>The Book of Revelation</u>
    a book which gives us a continual recapitulation
        of this present church age
            giving general principles for the church
            as well as details of God's work in history
            with the clear and undeniable theme
                that Christ will defeat His enemies
<u>The 24th Chapter of Matthew</u>
    the material of this chapter
        weaves together
            two great future events
            the fall of Jerusalem in 70 AD
            the events surrounding and including
                the Second Coming of Christ
                at the end of the age
<u>The 9th Chapter of Daniel</u>
    in verses 24-27 Daniel gives six insights
        as to what will take place
            at the first coming of Christ

as the history of Israel is given
in a period of 490 years or 70 weeks
with all of it being fulfilled
between Daniel's time
and the events surrounding
the death of Christ

The Rapture
The rapture of the church takes place
at the end of the tribulation period
which takes place at the end of this age
as all the bodies of all men are raised
to appear before one general judgment
of all men
who ever lived on this earth

The Post-Millennial View (Preterists)

The Millennium
the 1000 years are a symbolic figure
which signify a time of universal peace
of some years
upon the earth
which will be produced
by the preaching of the gospel
Christ will then come
at the end of this millennium
after the world has been Christianized

The Second Coming
a literal return of Christ
not to rule but set in motion
all of the final events of history
which will culminate in the eternal state

The Book of Revelation

a book which gave to the early church a prophecy
of the fall of Jerusalem in 70 AD
and all the accompanying horrors
when Titus and the Roman army
conquered the city of Jerusalem
many of this view believe (partial preterists)
that the Second Coming of Christ
is not in chapter 19---that concerns Jerusalem
but in chapter 20
some of this view (the full preterists) believe
that the book of Revelation does not mention
any Second Coming of Christ

The 24th Chapter of Matthew

the material of this chapter speaks primarily
of things which will take place
during the generation living at the time of Christ
thus it speaks of the fall of Jerusalem in 70 AD
as the city fell to Titus and the Roman army

The 9th Chapter of Daniel

in verses 24-27 Daniel gives a summary
of the history of the nation of Israel for the future
as she finishes her transgression against God
by rejecting Christ
as she stores up judgment for her sins
of the work of Christ
in atoning for sin
in bringing in everlasting righteousness
in fulfilling the prophecies concerning Himself
in the anointing of Christ as the Most Holy
thus there is no gap between the 490 years of prophecy
but all shall be fulfilled
at the first advent of Christ

I did come to another conclusion at this point. That even though we had not studied all the aspects of each view of prophecy (there seems to be no end), if one will study these areas carefully and deeply, that person could then decide which view he was convinced was Biblical.

That is not to say that my book with this material had said everything there was to say about even these areas. But it was to say that my book could, hopefully, give people a guidance as to what to look for in these key passages, and then from these considerations build thereon.

I still had a few things I wanted to do, but I sensed that for the most part, my book was finished in its essential content.

I was also convinced of another point, as I sat back and stretched. My search for my father was at another dead end! The Brandon Phillips name and book had given me no clue as to who my father really was, and unless the Lord undertook, the search was over.

So when Dink came by to invite me to go to Seminary City with him to get some books at the seminary library for his dissertation (yes, old Dink was still working on another degree), and, especially, when he offered to buy my lunch, I was more than eager and willing to ditch the pursuit and the study to go with him.

What could possibly happen to me at Seminary City that would drag me back into either one of these pursuits?

40

Can We Agree on the Second Coming?

As Dink and I made our way to seminary city, I found myself sermonizing on the subject of eschatology---why do people get so upset with one another when they find they disagree---sometimes over small matters?

I suggested to him that we list some principles concerning the Second Coming of Christ that whereby Christians who hold various views could find strong agreement. I began to list them as follows;

1. The doctrine of the Second Coming should cause our hearts to rejoice because we all would agree that Christ is coming back physically, bodily, visibly, suddenly, and gloriously.

2. As we study this doctrine, we should focus on Him, and not on minute intricate details, demanding that all agree with us, or we will not fellowship with them.

3. As we study this doctrine, we should study it humbly and graciously, not academically and theoretically, seeking to apply that which we learn to our hearts and lives in a manner that it will lead us to godly, Christ-like living.

4. Thus we should be able to judge our hearts as to whether or not we are studying this doctrine

correctly, as we see what attitude it is producing in us---humility, graciousness, love for Christ and others, worship, praise and adoration, or pride, sharpness of attitude, loss of love for Christ for others, division, grieving of a spirit of worship, and vile passions rather than godly passions.

5. Thus we should be able to judge our actions as to how this study affects us, as we see whether we have a pride of our knowledge, longing to be able to out-argue others, become offended because others cannot see it the way we do, and feel a sense of superiority because we have it all put together (we think) in a fullness of knowledge from which others must draw and agree.

6. Are there not some key ideas that all views should see alike and emphasize?

   a. Christ is the only Savior and only Lord who will come back someday in power and great glory to defeat and judge all of His enemies with an eternal separation from Him, and to bless and reward all His saints with an eternal presence with Him.

   b. God's people in the meantime should live holy and godly lives preaching the truth to every creature and to every corner of the earth whether the lost world around us receives or rejects the gospel, or whether they receive or reject us or even kill us.

    c. God's people should be ready and watching for His coming, because it will make no difference if we are perfect in our interpretation of Biblical prophecy if we are not ready for His coming. All the expertise and knowledge will be to no avail, if we are found wanting in the day of His coming.

    d. The enemy is the devil, not other Christians, and our energy and efforts should be forged against him, not against other Christians with whom we may disagree in these areas of Bible prophecy.

7. That there are some views that would set one in a camp of heresy, such as the following, though we cannot possibly give a complete list:

    a. To deny Christ is coming back
    b. To deny Christ is coming back bodily
    c. To deny Christ is coming back victoriously
        over all His enemies
            whether men or angels or demons
            whether Satan and all his power
    d. To believe that anyone can state the day or hour
    e. To believe that His coming will not include
        the resurrection of the lost to their eternal damnation
        nor the resurrection of the saved to their glorification and His eternal presence

It is amazing how quick a trip can pass, when one is busy, thinking and talking about our Lord and His glorious victory at the end of this age. Maranatha!

41

Can You Ever Forgive Me?

We arrived at the seminary library, and having nothing else to do, I decided I would wander through the stacks of books, to see if there was anything new to note. I headed for the prophetic books, and started scanning them, not really looking for anything, when suddenly there it was again---a copy of Brandon Phillips book. It had the same cover---maybe a few differences. But clearly, it was the same book, or was it? In God's providence it had been left on a shelf face up, and not in the stacks with the other books.

As I reached for it, I concluded I must have made a mistake, because it had the name Avery on it, and not Phillips But again, the cover and binding was almost exactly like the Phillip's book. I opened it, and saw again that many of the charts (not all) were the same as my father's original book, and again, were the same as they were in the Phillip's book. What was going on here, and who was the Avery guy.

Quickly, I turned to the title page, but I couldn't believe what I saw there! The author was Dr. Steven Avery, the past president of the seminary, the man who was pressured to resign in the inerrancy battle, which had gone on at the school, just a few years ago.[1] Though we had disagreed doctrinally (he was neo-orthodox in his view of Scripture), I had found him to be a gentleman in every way, and he seemed to have a special affection for me as well! I felt like I lost a true friend when he died shortly after he resigned as president under the pressure of the trustees.

I flipped over to the copyright page and saw that the book had been published in 1972. I shook my head as I considered the possible implications of what I had found. Could it be? Could it really be? I couldn't believe it!!

Either Dr. Steven Avery had plagiarized my father's work, or he was my father!!!!! Could it be that he had published his book in the fifties as a pre-mil under his real name of Ira Pointer, and then changed it to an a-mil view, and published it in the sixties under the pen name of Brandon Phillips, and then republished it in the seventies under his final assumed name of Steven Avery? But even more unbelievable, could he really be my father? How could I be sure?

I decided that there was only one way to be positive, and that was to go see his wife. Maybe she knew, and maybe she didn't! But I had to go and ask her---now.

I shared my find with Dink, who stood there and said what I had thought, "Wow!! Dat's unbelievable! Dr. Avery was yer dad?"

I was careful to warn Dink not to jump to conclusions, and with that mindset, we set off to find Mrs. Avery.

I learned that she still lived in the city, and thus with the book in hand, having checked it out, we made our way to her home. By the time we got there, butterflies had invaded my stomach, and I didn't know if I could go through with this without losing the lunch Dink had bought me. But we paused and prayed at the curb, and then made our way to the front door.

I knocked, then waited nervously, not knowing what I would do if she wasn't home, or what I would say if she was home. I couldn't wait another day, hour or second to find out if my life-long pursuit was finally over!

Finally, she opened the door, and I could tell by the way she was taken back at my presence, that she knew why I was there.

"Ira, please come in!" she said, as she began to cry, and that soon broke me up as well, to say nothing of the way Dink wept.

"I know why you are here, and I have a letter for you." she explained.

"For me? From Dr. Avery?" I asked, not wanting to press her too hard.

"Yes, from Dr. Avery---YOUR FATHER!"

Those were the words I had waited years to hear---your father! Could I have misunderstood her?

"Did I hear you right, Mrs. Avery. Did you say that Dr. Avery was my father? Really? Can I really believe that, after all these years of searching? And after that year of knowing him, and his knowing me, and he never told me?"

"Believe me, Ira, your father came home each night after meeting you, and being with you, and wept, sometimes into the wee hours of the morning, trying to decide if he should tell you. But he was afraid!" she explained.

"Afraid of what? Afraid of me?" I asked.

"Oh, son, he so enjoyed your company. To be able to see the kind of a young man of God you turned out to be, after he had failed you and your mother so miserably, was the greatest thrill and joy of his life. He couldn't say enough about you, and the friendship you both enjoyed together. You were all that he knew he should have been, and even wanted to be. Several times he talked of getting up the nerve to tell you, but each time he feared you would not understand, and that you would reject him."

"Reject him? I would never have done that!"

"But he didn't know that for sure, and he was full of fear, and so he continued to enjoy your fellowship, though his heart was breaking to tell you. Why he told me, that he could not imagine a son who could make him prouder and happier than you. And before he died, he wrote this letter, and told me to give it to you if you ever found out and came seeking the answer. He loved you so much, that he didn't want to risk losing you, now that you had found each other."

"But I did not know we had found each other?" I protested! "Why could I not have enjoyed the relationship as he did? Did not the lack of knowledge deprive me of the aching and yearnings of a young boy and man's life---to know his father? Was it not selfish of him to know what he knew, and yet never share it with me? Was not that the pattern of his whole life---a selfishness which he had never faced?"

She began to cry again, but through the tears, she urged me to read the letter. So I opened the letter and read:

My dear beloved son:

I have written this letter to you many times in my heart through the years. During those days when I was making so many mistakes and so full of sin and self; during those days in jail when I was running from God; during those months after getting my life straightened out. I have asked myself many times, how a father could treat a son like I have treated you. Even when I knew who you were, and didn't tell you, I failed you!!

Yet, I have found out that our God is a gracious God, and that though I have failed, He has molded you and shaped you into a servant for Him in a manner, that perhaps, I could not have done.

You are strong in the Lord, a man of conviction (which I was not so many times in my life). You are straightforward and honest, and do not possess a selfish bone in your body (Oh, how you put me to shame in so many ways by your godliness and Christ likeness).

How many times I wanted to tell you my secret, but I was afraid that you would see right through me to the wretch and hypocrite that I had been, and even was in some ways, as I knew who you were, and failed to tell you. Can you find it in your heart to forgive me?

And can I share another secret of my heart? When you taught those classes on the full authority of Scripture, and held the glory of God's person so high, my heart warmed anew as it had in those early days of ministry, and even in those first two years of your life, as our family was still together. Those were the happiest years of my life, when we were a family--- days when I was on fire for my God, like you are today, with a full confidence in Him and His Word.

Yes, your teaching and commitment to Christ drove me to my knees in despair and confession of sin. Oh, how I wished I could go back and relive my life! Back to that day I left His Word! Back to that day I drove you and your mother from me! Back to that day I came to her home town and kidnapped you! Back to that day when I put you in an orphanage to spite her! Back to those days when I wandered as a con man, even to find myself in jail! Back to the day when I made a new life, and then never came to look for you! Back to the day when God brought us together, and yet I said nothing about my true identity!

If you wonder how I could ever have treated you and your mother as I did, I have no excuses. My pride and arrogance of intellect, led me to think I knew more than God, and to believe I could plan and carry out my life without Him. But believe me, I paid for it. And I think the greatest price was my loss of you. I never saw you grow up, never got to play ball with you, never got to teach you, and never saw our hearts bind together as father and son. I am the loser, and I know you are a loser as well because of me, and I am so sorry!

My eyes are like Jeremiah's now, as I weep, not for the sins of the people, but for my own sins against you and my God. Please forgive me, and share these words of repentance and sorrow with your mother, if you ever find her. My dying prayer will be that someday you and she will be able to reunite, and that you will know the love she had for you, when I so cruelly separated you from her. And please, share my love to her, and my sorrow and repentance for the way I treated her.

Your loving father who is so proud of you.

Tears flooded my eyes as I read it, and mixed emotions flowed into my heart. But still all the questions had not yet been answered.

42

Was There True Repentance?

After the initial shock wore off, and we were able to sit and talk without crying, I addressed many of my remaining questions to Mrs. Avery.

My first question concerned Dr. Avery's (my father's) life history. What had happened to him after he left me at the orphanage? Part of the answer was known to me, and part was not.

First, after changing his identity for the first time in 1950 to Brandon Phillips, he fell in with the con men crowd in California (the ones who sought to con us). And as we knew already, they were soon in jail. I assumed then that Barwell and Flagler were being honest with us, when they told us that this is when and how they learned about me and my mother, and so many details of our lives.

When he got out of jail in 1952, he sought to separate himself from these "lewd fellows of the baser sort" (to use a good Biblical expression from Acts 17:5). That is when he changed his name and identity to Steven Avery. He went back to school under that name, and finished a bachelor's degree (even though he had one already under the name of Ira Pointer), and then a master's (again, even though he had one already). By 1960 he had earned a doctorate in an amazingly short amount of time. His graduate work was done at the Evangelistic Baptist Seminary in Seminary City! In the process he became a teaching assistant, then a full-fledged faculty member, and finally the president of the school in 1968.

As she spoke, I remembered Pastor Townsend's counsel to look for him at the top, as my father wanted the influence, prestige and power, which only the top would bring to him. Plus, he had the personality, knowledge and drive to get there. And he had also said, that either my father was at the top, or he had died trying to get there.

Concerning his books, it was during the sixties that he published his book under the pen name of his old identity of Brandon Phillips. He didn't dare, he thought, publish it under the name of Steven Avery. Later, feeling more secure, he did publish it under his final name of Steven Avery, especially since neither of the first two editions had sold many copies.

But this did not explain everything! I still had trouble with the fact that he never had looked for me, which Mrs. Avery admitted was true. Further, even when he met me, he not only did not tell me his identity, but he did not, even in some anonymous manner, inform me as to where I might find my mother. He certainly knew her hometown, and could have guided me in the right direction, even if he did not have a specific address.

For these failures she had no explanation, except to say that he was protecting his identity and position at the seminary. This led me to conclude that he died as he had lived---still self-centered, protecting himself, not really seeking to get all matters right with God. It is true, that the unexpected heart attack that killed him came immediately, and thus there was no opportunity to deal with these matters. But what about all the previous years of subterfuge in the living of a lie? Does not true repentance lead to the desire to make things right?

I must admit that I had some real doubts about his relationship with Christ, in light of such lack of any evidence of true repentance. I had to wonder if it was the continuation of a life of self-centeredness in the cloak of Christianity and Christian ministry. I hated to think and harbor such thoughts, and it was not because of any bitterness from my heart, but it was the truth of God's Word. True repentance results in a change of life, not in the direction to cover up one's sin with a new identity and name, but in the uncovering of one's past sin, and a breaking with it, and making past sin right, not only with God, but with one's fellow man. I wondered how a man who lived such a lie all those years, thinking only of himself in such a blatant manner, could truly be a follower of the Lord Jesus Christ!

After this discussion, and after prayer, Dink and I left Mrs. Avery, assuring her that we would seek to keep in touch. She and Dr. Avery did not have any children, and I thought that we might keep in touch and encourage her in the Lord.

For the first half of the trip home, there was silence, as Dink saw the need to let me stew in my thoughts. Finally I spoke.

"Well, Dink, its over, and I am glad! I feel drained and disappointed, and yet relieved and full! Does that make sense?"

"Yeah, Preacha, it does. What I wants ta know is if anybody at da seminary is goin' to announce dat Dr. Avery is yer father?"

"No, I doubt it, because only you, me, my mother, Mrs. Avery, and a few others are going to know about it. I would never want to use it for any personal advancement, nor would I want to ruin the reputation of another."

Little did I realize then, that I soon would be contacted by the seminary!

43

Postscript

A few weeks later I was shocked when I received a certain phone call. It was from the dean of faculty of the seminary. He wanted to know if I would consider joining the faculty of the Evangelistic Baptist Theological Seminary! I had already finished a masters program there, and was into the doctoral studies. They wanted me to teach theology, while I finished my doctoral work!

My first response was to ask why they were considering me for such a position! I didn't know, but I wondered if it had anything to do with who my father was! I had tried to keep all my father's past as quiet as possible, but it did leak out that he was my father. The dean answered, that since the school had gone conservative, they were in need of replacing certain faculty members, and that I had distinguished myself both in and out of the classroom.

I asked what the procedure would be, and he replied that, first, I would need to meet with the trustee committee, which was responsible for recommending the hiring of faculty members. Then with their full recommendation, if that were the case, my name would go to the whole board of trustees. With that approval, I would join the faculty, if I accepted the position.

My next question was with some humor, remembering my past experience in faculty hiring, when no theological questions were asked.

"Will they ask me about my theological views?"

I thoroughly expected to be grilled in all areas.

"Yes, you will be questioned!" the dean assured me.

I asked for time to pray about the matter. I wondered about the future of the church I was pastoring, and of Dink, and his family. It was agreed that I would be back in touch after a week of allowance for prayer concerning the matter.

When the conversation ended, I sat back and smiled, with some humor again in my mind.

I wondered if they would ask, "Young man, are you a Calvinist?"

Or maybe they would ask, "Young man, are you filled with the Holy Spirit?"

Or again, maybe they would ask, "Young man, what do you believe should be the Biblical government of a local church?"

I hoped they would ask, "Young man, do you believe in the verbal inspiration of the Bible?"

Then I laughed out loud. What would I say if they asked, "Young man, are you a pre-millennialist? Or an a-millennialist? Or a post-millennialist?"

I thought, "Maybe I need to make a study of that subject!"

Bibliography

Adams, Jay E., *I Will Tell You a Mystery* (Perspective Press, 1966). An a-mil preterist view, and well done.

Allis, Oswald T., *Prophecy and the Church* (Presbyterian and Reformed, 1945). An examination of the dispensational claim that the church is a parenthesis between the Old Testament promises of a kingdom to Israel and the final fulfillment of those promises.

Archer, Gleason L, Jr., Paul D. Feinberg, Douglas J. Moo, and Richard R. Reiter, *Three Views on the Rapture---Pre-, Mid-, or Post-?* (Zondervan, 1984). An excellent presentation and interaction of the three views of the rapture.

Blasing, Craig A., and Darrell L. Bock, *Progressive Dispensationalism* (Victor Books, 1993). The book carries a sub-title of "an up-to-date handbook of contemporary dispensational thought." This view sees (1) Christ ruling now in heaven, and yet to rule in the future on earth, (2) The new covenant blessings both now and future; (3) And one purpose of God in history.

Boettner, Loraine, *The Millennium* (Presbyterian and Reformed, 1957. A presentation by a post-mil of all the millennial views, post-mil, a-mil and pre-mil

Boice, James Montgomery, *The Last and Future World* (Zondervan). A pre-mil presentation.

Bray, John L., *Matthew 24 Fulfilled* (John L. Bray Ministry, Inc., 1996). A preterist view of Matthew 24.

Clouse, Robert G., *The Meaning Millennium: Four Views* (Intervarsity Press, 1977). A presentation of four eschatological views---historic pre-millennialism, dispensational pre-millennialism, post-millennialism, and a-millennialism.

Clouse, Robert G, and Robert N. Hosack, land Richard V. Pierard, *The New Millennium Manual---A Once and Future Guide* (Baker,

1999). This is termed as "...a popular guide to the issues, people, movements relevant to the coming Big Calendar Turn." The book does deal with millennial issues, among other subjects.

Cox, William E., *Amillennialism Today* (Presbyterian and Reformed, 1966). Obviously an a-mil view, and a good presentation of that view.

Crenshaw, Curtis I., and Grover E. Gunn III, *Dispensationalism--- Today, Yesterday and Tomorrow* (Footstool Publications, 1986). A critique of dispensationalism.

Enick, Douglas J., *When Will These Things Be?* (Brentwood Christian Press, 1998). One of the clearest presentations of the preterist view of Matthew 24.

Erickson, Millard J. *Contemporary Options in Eschatology* (Baker, 1977). This book was also published by the same publisher in 1998 under the title *A Basic Guide to Eschatology*. A good presentation with critique of the millennial views and also the tribulational views.

Gentry, Kenneth L., Jr., *Before Jerusalem Fell---Dating the book of Revelation* (American Vision, 1998). The author argues for the dating of the book of Revelation prior to AD 70 or the fall of Jerusalem.

Gentry, Kenneth L., Jr., and Thomas Ice, *The Great Tribulation---Past or Present?* (Kregel, 1999). A preterist view verses a dispensational view.

Gentry, Kenneth L., Jr., *He Shall Have Dominion* (Institute for Christian Economics, 1997). A theonomic, post-mil, preterist view. Gentry is doing some of the clearest writing concerning the preterist convictions.

Gentry, Kenneth L, Jr., *Perilous Times---A Study in Eschatological Evil* (Covenant Media Press, 1999). A preterist discussion of key eschatological passages, such as Daniel 9, Matthew 24, II Thessalonians 2, Revelation 13, and Revelation 17.

Grenz, Stanley J., *The Millennial Maze* (Intervarsity Press, 1992). An analysis of three millennial views---post-mil, a-mil, historic pre-mil, and dispensational pre-mil.

Gundry, Robert H., *The Church and the Tribulation* (Zondervan, 1973). A presentation of the post-tribulational view of the rapture.

Hoyt, Herman A., *The End Times* (Moody Press, 1969). A work which seeks to present various views, but clearly comes out in the dispensational pre-mil camp.

Ice, Thomas, and Kenneth L. Gentry, Jr., *The Great Tribulation---Past or Future* (Kregel---1999). Presentation of and dialogue between the futurist and preterist positions.

Kik, J. Marcellus, *An Eschatology of Victory* (Presbyterian and Reformed, 1971). A post-mil presentation of the key passages of eschatological study.

Kimball, William R., *The Rapture* (Baker, 1985). A critique of the pre-tribulational rapture view.

Ladd, George E., *The Blessed Hope* (Eerdmans, 1956). A historic pre-mil study of the second coming and the rapture.

Ladd, George E., *Crucial Questions about the Kingdom of God* (Eerdmans, 1952). An historic pre-mil discussion of the kingdom of God.

Ladd, George E., *The Gospel of the Kingdom* (Eerdmans, 1973) An historic pre-mil exposition of the key issues of the kingdom.

Ladd, George E., *Revelation* (Eerdmans, 1972). A historic pre-mil view of the book of Revelation.

Larkin, Clarence, *Dispensational Truth* (Clarence Larkin, 1918). The dispensational chart bible.

Lloyd-Jones, Martyn, *The Church and the Last Things* (Crossway Books, 1998). The author deals with all the millennial views in a very fair and readable manner.

Mathison, Keith A., *Dispensationalism---Rightly Dividing the People of God* (Puritan and Reformed, 1995). A Reformed critique of the dispensational view.

Mathison, Keith A., *Postmillennialism---An Eschatology of Hope* (Presbyterian and Reformed, 1999). A more recent presentation of the post-mil preterist of the key passages of the eschatological search.

McClain, Alva J., *Daniel's Prophecy of the 70 Weeks* (Zondervan, 1969). A pre-mil exposition of Daniel 9.

Pate, C. Marvin, General Editor, *Four Views on the Book of Revelation* (Zondervan, 1998). A presentation of the following views by the following authors: Preterist, Kenneth L. Gentry, Jr.; Idealist, Sam Hamstra, Jr.; Progressive Dispensationalist, C. Martin Pate; Classical Dispensationalism, Robert L. Thomas. An excellent introduction to the various views of Revelation.

Pentecost, J. Dwight, *Things to Come* (Dunham Publishing, 1958). This is the classic dispensational pre-mil bible.

Poythress, Vern S., *Understanding Dispensationalists* (Zondervan, 1987). An attempt at dialogue between dispensationalism and covenant theology.`

Rosenthal, Marvin, *The Pre-wrath Rapture of the Church* (Thomas Nelson, 1990). Presents a new understanding of the tribulation, with the rapture being sometime during the second half of the tribulation period, prior to the opening of the seventh seal of the book of Revelation.

Russell, J. Stuart, *The Parousia---The New Testament Doctrine of Our Lord's Second Coming* (Baker, 1983). An older writer's view of preterism.

Sproul, R. C., *The Last Days according to Jesus* (Baker, 1998). A preterist view of Matthew 24.

Thomas, Robert L., *Revelation---An Exegetical Commentary* in two volumes (Moody, 1995). This is the best and most scholarly commentary on the book of Revelation from a dispensational pre-mil view point.

Van Kampen, Robert, *The Rapture Question Plain and Simple* (Revell, 1997). A pre-wrath presentation of the rapture.

Walsworth, Keith and Kenneth Hill, *What's Next?---A Non-biased Study of Eschatology* (Hearthstone Publishing, 1993). A good presentation and summary of the various eschatological views---a-mil, post-mil, historic pre-mil and dispensational pre-mil, with critique of each view except the dispensational view.

Walvoord, John F., *The Blessed Hope and the Tribulation* (Zondervan, 1976). The author examines the post-trib view of the rapture from his pre-trib convictions.

Walvoord, John F., *Daniel---The Key to Prophetic Revelation* (Moody Press, 1971). A dispensational presentation of the book of Daniel.

Walvoord, John F., *The Millennial Kingdom* (Zondervan, 1959). The author presents a thorough discussion of the three millennial views with critique.

Walvoord, John F., *The Rapture Question* (Zondervan, 1979). The author presents a dispensational pre-trib view of the rapture.

Willis, Wesley R., and John R. Master, Editors, *Issues in Dispensationalism* (Moody, 1994). This book is the answer of the classic dispensationalists to the current-day progressive dispensationalists.

Wood, Leon J., *The Bible and Future Events* (Zondervan, 1973). The author gives a brief survey of the last day events from a pre-mil pre-trib view.

LIST OF RICHBARRY PRESS BOOKS
DR. RICHARD P. BELCHER
Richbarry Press, Box 302, Columbia, SC 29202
Phone: 803-750-0408
Fax: 803-798-3190
E-mail: docbelcher@juno.com
For prices see our web site: richbarrypress.com

THEOLOGY

A Comparison of Dispensationalism and Covenant Theology 46 pages   ISBN # 0-925703-52-4   An objective analysis and comparison of two major systems of theology.

A Layman's Guide to the Lordship Controversy 123 pages   ISBN # 0-925703-13-3   In this work the author aids the layman in coming to an understanding of the controversy by summarizing the two positions on this important issue---the Lordship and non-lordship views. He then provides an excellent critique of the non-lordship position based on Scripture.

A Layman's Guide to the Sabbath Question 161 pages   ISBN # 0-925703-43-5   Co-authored by Richard P. Belcher, Jr., this book presents and compares three current views of the Sabbath---The Seventh Day view, the Christian Sabbath view, and the Lord's Day view.

I Believe in Inerrancy 54 pages   ISBN # 0-925703-24-9   A Biblical, historical and theological presentation of the doctrine of the inspiration of the Scriptures especially prepared for the layman, but helpful to all.

GREEK HELPS

A Practical Approach to the Greek New Testament 52 Pages (8 1/2 by 11)   ISBN # 1-883265-03-7   An introduction to a practical use of the Greek NT helpful and useful for both those who have had Greek and those who have not.

Diagramming the Greek New Testament 62 pages (8 1/2 by 11) ISBN # 1-883265-06-1 A self-teaching manual to help one learn to diagram the Greek NT.

Doing an Effective Greek Word Study 23 pages A manual which charts the procedure for doing a Greek word study from the Classical, Hellenistic, Patriarchal, etc. sources.

Doing Textual Criticism in the Greek New Testament 25 pages A manual which explains in a simple and understandable manner the principles of doing textual criticism in the Greek New Testament.

Doing Biblical Exegesis 10 pages A manual which traces the basic steps in doing Biblical exegesis in a major or minor manner.

MINISTRY HELPS

Teaching Helps in Psalms 53 pages (8 1/2 by 11) ISBN # 1-883265-02-9 A doctrinal study guide of Psalms with a clear preachable or teachable outline which can be easily divided into individual outlines. Doctrinal areas covered include the Scriptures, God, man, worship, etc. Background material is presented also in an introductory ministry outline.

Ministry Helps in Isaiah 132 pages (8 1/2 by 11) ISBN# 1-883265-15-0 A study guide of Isaiah with a clear preachable or teachable outline which can easily be divided into separate outlines following the subjects of the sin of God's people, the judgment of God's people, the solution to the problem of God's people, the future blessings of God's people, etc. Background material is presented also in an introductory ministry outline.

Ministry Helps in Hosea 56 pages (8 1/2 by 11) ISBN # 1-883265-08-8 A study guide of Hosea with a clear preachable or teachable outline which can easily be divided into separate outlines. Background material is presented in the form of an introductory ministry outline.

Ministry Helps in Amos 48 pages (8 1/2 by 11) ISBN # 1-883265-16-9 A study guide of Amos with a clear preachable or teachable outline which can easily be made into separate outlines. Background material is in the form of an introductory ministry outline.

Teaching Helps in Malachi 38 pages (8 1/2 by 11) ISBN # 0-925703-63-X A study guide of Malachi with a clear preachable or teachable outline which can easily be divided into individual outlines following the theme of the burden of Malachi. Background material is presented also in an introductory ministry outline.

Teaching Helps in Luke 128 pages (8 1/2 by 11) ISBN # 1-883265-13-4 A study guide of Luke with a clear preachable or teachable outline which can easily be divided into individual outlines. Background material is presented in an introductory ministry outline.

Ministry Helps in John 60 pages (8 1/2 by 11) ISBN # 0-925703-18-4 A study guide of John with a clear preachable or teachable outline which can easily be divided into individual outlines following the theme of the Word Christ Jesus as presented, pondered, persecuted, etc. Background material is presented in an introductory ministry outline.

Ministry Helps in Acts 72 pages (8 1/2 by 11) ISBN # 0-925703-62-1 A study guide of Acts with a clear preachable or teachable outline which can easily be divided into outlines following the theme of six provisions God made for world evangelization. Background material is presented also in an introductory ministry outline.

Teaching Helps in I Corinthians (8 1/2 by 11) ISBN # 1-883265-04-5 A study guide of I Corinthians with a clear preachable or teachable outline which can easily be divided into individual outlines. The study addresses the many subjects and problems in the church at Corinth---divisions, Christian liberty, the gifts of the Spirit, etc. Background material is presented also in an introductory ministry outline.

Teaching Helps in II Corinthians (8 1/2 by 11) ISBN # 0-925703-15-X A study guide of II Corinthians with a clear preachable or teachable outline which can easily be divided into individual outlines following the theme of New Testament ministry. Background material is presented also in an introductory ministry outline.

Ministry Helps in Galatians (8 1/2 by 11)   ISBN # 1-883265-17-7
A study guide of Galatians with a clear preachable or teachable outline
which can easily be divided into separate outlines following the theme
of Paul's gospel. Background material is presented also in an
introductory ministry outline.

Ministry Helps in Ephesians (8 1/2 by 11)   ISBN # 1-883265-18-5
A study guide of Ephesians with a clear preachable or teachable outline
which can easily be divided into separate outlines following the theme
of the one body of Christ. Background material is presented also in an
introductory ministry outline.

Teaching Helps in Hebrews (8 1/2 by 11)   ISBN # 0-925703-16-8 A
study guide of Hebrews with a clear preachable or teachable outline
which can easily be divided into individual outlines following the
theme of the superiority of the New Covenant. Background material is
presented also in an introductory ministry outline.

Teaching Helps in James (8 1/2 by 11)   ISBN # 0-925703-17-6   A
study guide of James with a clear preachable and teachable outline
which can easily be divided into individual outlines following the
theme of practical Christian living. Background material is presented
also in an introductory ministry outline.

Teaching Helps in I Peter (8 1/2 by 11)   ISBN # 1-883265-05-3   A
study guide of I Peter with a clear preachable and teachable outline
which can easily be divided into individual outlines following the
theme of the covenant people of God---their blessings and
responsibilities.

SERMON HELPS---THEOLOGY AND METHOD

**Preaching the Gospel---A Theological Perspective And A Personal
Method** 120 pages   ISBN # 883265-10-X This work was formerly
published as two books. Using I Corinthians 1-4 and II Timothy 3:1-4
as the basis of study, the author sets forth the nature of the gospel we
must preach and the nature of the methods we must employ as we
preach it. In the second part of the work, the author sets forth a method

of preaching, including the matters of kinds of sermons, the organization of a sermon, the introduction, the body, the main points, the conclusion, the illustrations, the application, and the delivery of the sermon.

THEOLOGICAL NOVELS

A Journey in Grace   154 pages   ISBN # 0-925703-11-7   This is a theological novel---the story of a young pastor with a typical twentieth century theology, and his pursuit of a burning theological question, which is triggered in his first   experience with a pulpit search committee.   He cannot and does not rest until he has faced and answered the question, "Young man, are you a Calvinist?"

A Journey in Purity   215 pages   ISBN # 0-925703-39-7   This is the sequel to the novel *A Journey in Grace*.   It is the story of the same pastor in his difficult and heart-braking struggle to bring purity to the corrupt and impure church which he pastors.   This book identifies with any pastor or church member who has ever wrestled with the principles of church discipline, and their application to a local church, and the pain and difficulty in restoring the church to purity.

A Journey in Authority   183 pages   ISBN # 1-883265-11-8   This continues the series of journey books.   It is the story of the same young pastor as he wrestles with the question of church government---congregational-rule versus elder-leadership, along with an attempt to solve a strange mystery threatening the life of one of his members.

A Journey in the Spirit   240 pages   ISBN # 1-883265-12-6   This continues Pastor Ira Pointer's search for truth---this time in the area of the doctrine of the Holy Spirit.   By the meeting of a strange and unique individual, who asks him if he has   been filled with the Spirit, he finds himself in the swirl of the modern Pentecostal-Charismatic movement. A shocking surprise ending unmasks the stranger and further opens his eyes to the truth.

A Journey in Inspiration   165 pages   ISBN # 1-883265-14-2 Pastor Pointer faces the inerrancy battle of the late 60's and early 70's as a student at seminary.   Attacked verbally and literally for his convictions about the Bible, he confronts unbelief in the classroom, cafeteria, newspaper and from a mysterious character called the "Strawman." This book is a must to understand the inerrancy debate of those decades, as well as so much more going on in the church today in belief and practice.

A Journey in Providence   208 pages   ISBN # 1-883-265-19-3   A tragedy in the family of one of the primary characters of the previous books in this series, opens not only a search for truth concerning the providence of God in life's trials, but also a search to solve the mysteries involved in the tragedy.   Unexpected twists and turns in the plot, as the author weaves a Biblical exposition of Job with humor, mystery and blessing, makes this a very readable and doctrinally informative book.

A Journey in Eschatology   217 pages   ISBN # 1-883265-21-5 Pastor Pointer is involved in two pursuits in this book---one in the theological area and the other in his personal life.   The theological pursuit comes from an invitation to write a book on eschatology, and the other comes as he is spurred to search for his birth parents, as he was reared in a children's home and has never been able to locate his mother and father.   Surprises of sorrow and of joy come as he finds his mother, but concludes he may never find the identity of his father.

HISTORICAL STUDIES

Seventeenth Century Baptist   Confessions of Faith   56 pages ISBN # 0-925703-23-0   Co-authored by Anthony Mattia, this is a discussion and refutation of a modern day claim that the First London Confession in its 1644 and 1646 editions has a different view of the Law than the Second London Confession of 1689.

BOOKS ABOUT A. W. PINK

A. W. Pink---Predestination   136 pages   ISBN # 0-925703-51-6   An analysis and critique of the central theological theme of A. W. Pink. This work uses the Pink sources to set forth his views of predestination, election and reprobation.

A. W. Pink---Born to Write   165 pages   ISBN # 1-883265- 01-1 This is the second edition of a biography of Pink which first appeared in 1982. The author not only presents the facts of Pink's life, with several chapters of new material possessed by no other biographer, but he also analyzes the life of Pink---his unique personality, his rejection by men, his study methodology, his withdrawal, and his life of isolation during his final years.

Arthur W. Pink---Letters from Spartanburg 1917-1920   287 pages ISBN # 1-883265-00-2   A series of about a hundred letters written by Pink when he was pastor of the Northside Baptist Church in Spartan burg, SC 1917-1920. This is the time he wrote his best known book, *The Sovereignty of God.* Edited by Dr. Belcher with a complete index for easy use.

Arthur W. Pink---Letters of an Itinerant Preacher 1920-1921   93 pages   ISBN # 1-883265-09-6   A series of letters written by Pink when he was an itinerant preacher working mostly in the state of California. This was a period when he was wrestling with God's will for his life, whether to continue a public ministry or devote himself exclusively to a writing ministry. Edited by Dr. Belcher with a complete index for easy use.

REPRINTS OF OLDER BOOKS

Luther Rice---Pioneer in Missions and Education   125 pages   ISBN # 1-883265-07-X   This is an old biography of Luther Rice by Edward B. Pollard and Daniel Gurden Stevens, first published in the early part of the twentieth century. It details the life of Rice and the strong, but sometimes unknown contribution, he made to the cause of modern missions and education in the life of Baptists of America. The book was prepared for publication by Richard P. Belcher.